Campbell, Hutson, and Sharp's

Great Smoky Mountains
Wildflowers

5th edition

**prepared by Robert W. Hutson,
William F. Hutson, and Aaron J. Sharp**

**Additional photographs by
Alan S. Heilman and Kitty Kohout**

**Windy Pines Publishing
Northbrook**

Dedication

This edition is dedicated to the memory of our deceased co-author Carlos C. Campbell. Mr. Campbell was intimately associated with the early efforts to establish a National Park in the Smokies and subsequently devoted more than fifty years to the conservation and promotion of the beauties of nature in order to insure its protection for future generations.

Acknowledgements

As with any book, many individuals provided support in its creation and we are grateful to them all. Special thanks go to Glenn Cardwell, Supervisory Ranger, now retired, for his assistance both in the identification and location of many of the wildflowers. Thanks also to: Don DeFoe, Assistant Chief of Visitor Services; Nelson Wilkins, Seasonal Ranger; Annette Hartigan, Park Librarian; Lucinda Ogle, Wildflower Pilgrimage co-founder; Dr. Eugene Wofford and Dr. Alan Heilman of The University of Tennessee Botany Department; Joseph Bowlby, the book's designer; Mary Hutson, Margret Orr, Mary Root, and Donna Lane for their encouragement and help.

We also wish to express our appreciation to Glenn and Faye Cardwell for their review of the draft manuscript and helpful suggestions.

Special thanks goes to Arthur Stupka first Park Naturalist, now retired, for his assistance in the early days and to the late Louis Iglehart, first Editor of the UT Press, who shared our dream and vision of a book for the Park Visitor that continues now more than 30 years later in this 5th edition. Thanks also to the Great Smoky Mountains Conservation Association for its financial assistance in publication of the second edition.

copyright © 1962, 1964, 1970, 1977, 1994, 1995 by Robert W. Hutson

photographs first appearing in 5th edition © 1995
by Robert W. or William F. Hutson as indicated by photo credits
except: American Holly © 1995 Kitty Kohout/Root Resources

Published by
Windy Pines Publishing
2755 Pfingsten Rd
Northbrook, IL 60062

L.C. Catalog Card #95-61682
ISBN 0-9643417-3-5
Pre-press in U.S.A.
Printed in Hong Kong

_S_tarting before the winter's snows have melted and continuing well into late autumn, there is a gay and colorful procession of wildflowers in the Great Smoky Mountains National Park. The luxuriant, highly varied vegetation of these mountains includes approximately 1,500 species of native flowering herbs, shrubs, and trees. In fact, the Park could appropriately be called "The Wildflower National Park." As Arthur Stupka, who for 25 years was Park Naturalist in the Smokies, says, "Vegetation to the Great Smoky Mountains National Park is what granite domes and waterfalls are to Yosemite, geysers are to Yellowstone, and sculptured pinnacles are to Bryce Canyon National Park."

The richness of flora is one of its most distinctive features, the Park's diverse environments having provided niches for the survival of many plant species. Situated in one of the oldest mountain masses, the area has not been covered by marine waters nor glacial ice. Here persist a few members of subtropical families which were much better represented in preglacial times. Associated with them are northern types which probably migrated southward during the glacial epoch.

The venerable age of the mountains is only one of several factors which contribute to the great variety of wildflowers and other plant life. Other influences include variations in elevation, rainfall, nature and slope of the rocks, and temperature.

Elevations, for instance, range from 857 feet at the junction of Abrams Creek and Little Tennessee River up to the highest peak in the Park, Clingmans Dome at 6,643 feet.

Rainfall sometimes exceeds 100 inches a year in the spruce-fir forests on and near the summits. The average for the upper elevations in general is 85 inches, whereas 50 inches a year is more common in the foothills. Thus it is that we find certain types of plants prospering on the drier slopes of the lower elevations and other kinds thriving in the abundant rainfall common to the upper elevations.

Temperatures are influenced by the wide range in elevations. The mountaintops usually are about 10 to 20 degrees

3

cooler than the Park foothills. This has an important bearing on the fact that you can find almost as many kinds of flowering plants between the foothills and the peaks as you will see on a trip from the Great Smokies to Canada. Near the summits of several peaks are many species that are common in Canada, such as the yellow flowered Clinton's lily, wood sorrel, and witch-hobble. ❧

Flowers
That Moved Up

Nearly all of the flowers the visitor will see in the Great Smokies are native species. Likewise, most of those included in this book are indigenous to the Park.

However, there are a few species - usually found in the foothills of the Park and in the surrounding valley - that are now well established at much higher elevations. Man and nature assisted this upward movement by changing the vegetational cover in some manner, creating what we call "disturbed areas." Man disturbed the cover by removing trees and shrubs from old homesites and in building roads and trails. Nature created other changes with severe windstorms, landslides caused by cloudbursts, and occasionally fires caused by lightning.

It is possible that wind and birds carried seeds of the lowland plants to these fertile disturbed areas at higher elevations. It is more likely, however, that most of the plants "moved up" to their new environment by means of mulching material and grass seeds applied to road banks and shoulders. The disturbed areas, usually quite small in size, may be seen throughout the Park, and they have permitted certain beautiful flowers to be found at present locations in unusual abundance. On valley farms, some of the flowers are classed as weeds-a weed being a plant growing where it is not wanted. But, along the high elevation roads and trails the ox-eye daisy, the dandelion, and other such "weeds" are now adding touches of beauty. ❧

Finding Wildflowers
In The Smokies

A major purpose of this book is to tell *where* and *when* wildflowers may be found *in the Great Smokies*. The desire of the authors is to share with others not only the kaleidoscope of colors and the exquisite form of these flowers but also the thrill of discovery and identification. Such help to the flower lover is not possible in a more general wildflower book, which may treat several areas or even the entire country. Thus, special emphasis has been placed here on filling a unique need for the Smokies visitor by listing easily-found spots where each plant may be seen. In some instances, larger and more conspicuous displays can be found at other locations; but these usually are for the hardier walkers and climbers, who are invited to obtain further information from Park interpreters or rangers.

It should be added, too, that the delicate beauty of wildflowers is best revealed at very close range. A discerning eye is more important than miles traveled; frequently, only a short walk from the car is necessary to locate a plant. Many of the flower descriptions are intended to aid the close observer by telling of unusual features to look for.

Although interesting wildflowers may be found in the Great Smokies most of the year, there are two periods of unusual abundance: mid-April to mid-May, and mid-June to mid-July. The annual Wildflower Pilgrimages are held on the last Thursday, Friday, and Saturday of April timed to coincide with the first period. Participants have a choice of several trips each day, guided by botanists and other specialists, to areas where many wildflowers may be seen and photographed. Details about the Pilgrimages may be obtained from the Sugarlands Visitor Center, Gatlinburg, Tennessee 37738.

During the second period of special flowering abundance, mid-June to mid-July, the extravagant displays of mountain laurel, the rhododendrons, azaleas, and other heath shrubs are massed for the visitor. Park rangers also conduct frequent hikes to the special displays.

The Park's Self-Guiding Nature Trails, a mile or less in length, afford some of the best opportunities for you to find large numbers of wildflowers on your own. Strategically located in a variety of environments, these trails are virtually open-air botanical gardens.

The diversity of the Park's flora means, of course, that most of the wildflowers found in these mountains also occur elsewhere. Many grow along the nearby Foothills Parkway and the scenic Blue Ridge Parkway, and on up to Shenandoah National Park. Some will be found in distant sections of the

United States and even in other countries, but not necessarily at the same flowering season. ❧

Notes For The User
Of This Book

The wildflowers selected for presentation here are representative of the Park and surrounding region. The various flowers are grouped roughly in the order of their blooming season. The text is designed especially for the layman but is intended to be botanically accurate. For clarity, the word "fruits," as employed by botanists, is used in most cases instead of "berries" or "seeds." Elevation figures are averages based on common occurrence of the plant described, but it is possible to find a few flowers outside the indicated range. Where described verbally low corresponds roughly to below 2,500 feet, mid or middle to 2,500-4,500 feet, and high to over 4,500 feet.

The scientific names used are those which we believe the reader will find the most helpful. In some cases, they may not be the very latest name that distinction being transitory and somewhat dependent upon the opinion of a particular authority. Since many flower books follow the nomenclature in *Gray's Manual of Botany 8th Ed.* by Fernald, where *Gray's* significantly differs, the more modern name is shown first and *Gray's* follows in parenthesis. For a more technical treatment of our wildflowers *Gray's* will be helpful, as will the *New Britton & Brown Illustrated Flora* by Gleason, *Manual of the Vascular Flora of the Carolinas* by Radford, Ahles & Bell, *Manual of Vascular Plants 2nd Ed.* by Gleason & Cronquist, *Guide to the Vascular Plants of the Blue Ridge* by Wofford, *Flowering Plants of the Great Smoky Mountains* a checklist published by the Great Smoky Mountains Natural History Association and other texts. The source for the national champion trees living in the Park is the *1996-97 National Register of Big Trees* published by the American Forestry Association. This of course is subject to change as larger trees are discovered or existing giants fall prey to disease or storms.

Since the first edition of this book in 1962, our country has developed a greater awareness of our natural world. Our love of nature has created additional pressures on our wilderness areas. The Great Smoky Mountains National Park is visited by more than nine million people each year. Please stay on the trails and obey the Park rules. Within the Great Smoky

Mountains National Park anyone who picks, digs, or breaks any wildflower (or disturbs animal life) is subject to arrest. With so many visitors, even a very small percentage of law breaking "flower pickers" translates into massive destruction.

Our love of wildflowers has created an interest in wildflower gardens. Removing plants from the Park is strictly forbidden. Please use only nursery raised wildflowers from reputable growers. It is our belief that species which cannot be raised commercially should not be purchased. As with elephant ivory, the best way to stop the underground trafficking in these plants by the unscrupulous is to eliminate any legitimate market for them. In an article published in the Park's newspaper, the Park Service refers to a study plot of 200 lady's slippers that was reduced to 15 in a matter of five years. Poaching is believed to be a principal cause. Sadly because of their very unique habitat requirements, they most likely died after being transplanted. We recommend joining a native plant society or garden club. They can provide you with valuable information on the best species to grow and reputable suppliers.

The interest in folk remedies, foods, and other historical uses of native plants is creating additional pressures. Ginseng poaching, for example, is a major problem. Because many different plants look alike, simply matching a plant to a photograph or verbal description in a field guide is insufficient for absolute identification. Also, being natural doesn't make it safe. Some plants are actually poisonous if improperly used or prepared. Others, even when "properly" used and prepared, are now known to produce severe side effects. The details of the preparation and use of these plants are beyond the scope of this book. For your own safety and to protect our environment, these folk uses should be viewed as historical curiosities and not as something to try yourself.

Flower photographers at one time were a rarity on the trails. Today, in the spring, you are likely to see several amateur and professional photographers at any one time on popular nature trails. Remember, no photograph is worth damaging your subject or its environment.

It is our hope that the following camera and word pictures will help to enrich your visit to the Great Smoky Mountains National Park. ❧

The Authors

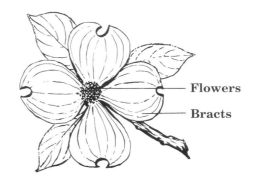

Flowers

Bracts

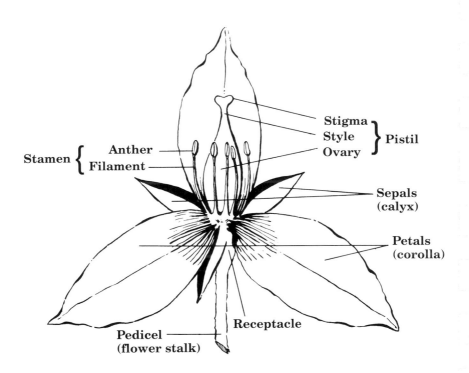

Stigma ⎤
Style ⎬ Pistil
Ovary ⎦

Stamen {
Anther
Filament

Sepals
(calyx)

Petals
(corolla)

Pedicel
(flower stalk)

Receptacle

Flower and Inflorescences

A flower as seen by a botanist is really a short stem terminated by whorls of modified leaves. The outermost set of "leaves" (the calyx) consists of sepals usually green in color. The next whorl above consists of petals (collectively the corolla) usually white or colored some shade other than green. Between the corolla and the pistil(s) are the stamens, each consisting of a filament, often erect, terminated by a head-like anther containing pollen. The tip (stigma) of the pistil is the part receptive to the pollen. It is apical on a stalk (style) which is borne on top of the ovary, the enlarged basal portion of the pistil, which may mature into a fruit. Within the fruits the seeds develop. All of the flower parts are attached to the apex (receptacle) of a stem (pedicel).

At times it is difficult to distinguish between a flower and a cluster (inflorescence) of flowers. In the flowering dogwood (see drawing at left) a group of small, inconspicuous flowers are surrounded by four large, white, special leaves (bracts). In the sunflower, small flowers in the center of the head are surrounded by much larger and more showy ray-flowers around the edge. In such instances, what appears to be a single flower is in reality a whole corsage, or bouquet. ❧

Spring Beauty
Claytonia virginica   Purslane family

With dainty and beautiful flowers with pink striped petals, spring beauty is fairly abundant at all elevations in the Smokies. It is one of the earliest to bloom-usually from late February through May. The narrow-leaved plants are frequently found mixed with the broad-leaved type, *C. caroliniana*, and many intermediate forms. Only 3 or 4 inches tall, spring beauty grows on rich, wooded slopes. A good place to find it is along the Appalachian Trail between Newfound Gap and Indian Gap. ❧

Sweet White Violet
Viola blanda   Violet family

One of three white violets often confused, this one is abundant in the foothills of the Smokies. At elevations of 4,000 to 5,000 feet it may be found along with northern white violet, *V. macloskeyi subsp. pallens (pallens)*, which does not have the upper two strongly bent back/twisted petals and reddish flower stalk normally present in *V. blanda*. The third white species, large leaved violet (*V. incognita* included in *V. blanda* by many), is rare and has bearded lateral petals. Sweet white violets grow in moist to wet, shaded, acid soils and bloom from March through June, along almost any brook above 2,500 feet elevation. ❧

Hepatica
Hepatica acutiloba   Buttercup family

The acute-leaved SHARP-LOBED HEPATICA is one of two species of the genus which adorns the trailsides in most deciduous woods at the lower elevations, and occurs up to 3,000 feet. The average height is 3 or 4 inches. Its flowers range from pure white through the pinks, blues, and purples. Exceptionally fine displays may be seen on the Cove Hardwood Nature Trail during March and April, depending on whether spring is early or late. Because of the shape of the hepatica leaf, people in the Middle Ages regarded it as a cure for liver ailments. The other species is round-lobed hepatica (*H. americana*) whose leaf has a rounded rather than a pointed leaf tip. ❧

Hairy Buttercup
Ranunculus hispidus   Buttercup family

The beautiful yellow flowers, about one inch in diameter, on hairy stems from 5 to 10 inches tall, occur mostly at elevations below 3,000 feet. They may be seen in the Little River Gorge from late March through April. Twelve other buttercup species are found in the Great Smokies. All have distinctive shiny, waxy yellow petals. ❧

10

Spring Beauty *R. Hutson photo*

Sweet White Violet *W. Hutson photo*

Hepatica *R. Hutson photo*

Hairy Buttercup *W. Hutson photo*

Trailing Arbutus
Epigaea repens — Heath family

This dwarf shrub is fairly common in sandy, acid soils from 1,000 to 4,000 feet elevation in the Great Smokies. It may be seen along the Abrams Falls Trail, the Bullhead Trail and occasionally at high elevations such as Andrews Bald (5,800 feet). All plants are protected by federal law in the Smokies and other national parks, but trailing arbutus is one of several plants also protected by law in many states. The delicately scented white to pink flowers, previously used as a perfume by some mountain women, appear from early March through late May. Its rare beauty has been heralded by some of our early poets. ❧

Round Leaved Violet
Viola rotundifolia — Violet family

This is our only early yellow violet which has flowers borne directly from the root stalk. The small flower is quite exquisite with brown veins and a lateral beard. The round leaves are fine toothed, and are often retained over the winter. This violet is common in March and April, occasionally blooming as late as July, in shaded moist soil and grows at elevations up to 5,000 feet. ❧

Dutchman's-breeches
Dicentra cucullaria — Fumitory family

This rather rare, distinctively shaped nodding flower, with spurs at the top, is found from 900 to 5,000 feet elevation in the Smokies. Because of the extended "trouser legs," it is sometimes called LITTLE BOY PLANT. The cream-white flowers appear in April and May, and may be found in the same locations listed below. The plant is very similar to and often intermixed with the related squirrel corn. ❧

Squirrel Corn
Dicentra canadensis — Fumitory family

This plant is very closely related to dutchman's-breeches and bleeding heart (p. 60), the flower being a white "version" of the latter. Because of the rounded or "bloomer-like" top of its flowers, it is occasionally called LITTLE GIRL PLANT. Squirrel corn gets its name from a belief that squirrels enjoy its corn-like tubers. The cream-white flowers appear in April and May at most all elevations often intermixed with dutchman's-breeches. It may be found in the Chimneys picnic area and along the Cove Hardwood Nature Trail and the Appalachian Trail between Newfound and Indian Gaps. ❧

Trailing Arbutus

R. Hutson photo

Round Leaved Violet

R. Hutson photo

Dutchman's-breeches
W. Hutson photo

Squirrel Corn
inset
R. Hutson photo

Bloodroot
Sanguinaria canadensis   Poppy family

This is one of the very early wildflowers, appearing from mid-March to mid-April. The clear white flowers, on stems about 8 inches tall, grow along the Cove Hardwood Nature Trail, the Roaring Fork Motor Nature Trail, the Porters Creek Trail and generally in moist, deciduous woods up to about 3,000 feet. The slender, oval petals normally drop off in one to three days. Interestingly, the flower stem rises through an open space at the base of the accompanying leaf. The root contains an orange-red sap, which accounts for the common name. ❧

Plantain-leaved Pussy's Toes
Antennaria plantaginifolia   Aster family

The sexes are separated on different plants in this species. This one happens to be a male. These plants can be found on trailsides at low to mid elevations in March though early May. They range from 2 to 24 inches in height tending towards the smaller. Another name for this plant is LADIES' TOBACCO. Of the three members of this genus in the Park it is the only one with multiple flower-heads and leaves with three or more veins. The others *A. solitaria* has only one flower-head and *A. neglecta* has only one vein. ❧

Fraser's Sedge
Cymophyllus fraseri   Sedge family

Its leathery, evergreen, drooping, iris shaped leaves are quite distinctive. The white cluster of male flowers are borne above the green cluster of female flowers. It is apparently a relic from the evolutionary past. Not common, it is found in moist ravines at lower elevations. The plant blooms in March through May and can be seen on the Grotto Falls and Porters Creek Trails. ❧

Smooth Yellow Violet
Viola pensylvanica   Violet family

Also known as PENNSYLVANIA VIOLET, this species is quite common in deciduous woods that are moist but well drained. Flowers appear in April and early May. The height ranges from 4 to 15 inches, depending on the fertility of the soil. It is widely distributed at elevations below 2,500 feet, but may be seen on the Cove Hardwood Nature Trail, as well as the Ramsay Cascades, and Porters Creek Trails. Some people now include this violet in *V. eriocarpa* or *pubescens*. ❧

14

Bloodroot *W. Hutson photo*

Plantain-leaved Pussy's Toes
R. Hutson photo

Fraser's Sedge *W. Hutson photo*

Smooth Yellow Violet *R. Hutson photo*

White Fringed Phacelia
Phacelia fimbriata   Waterleaf family

Only 3 to 5 inches tall, this *Phacelia* is noted for massing in large beds, sometimes covering almost an acre. From a distance, the beds resemble patches of snow. The plant is widely distributed at elevations from 2,500 to 5,000 feet and blooms in April and May. An easily accessible location for viewing is the entrance to Chimneys Picnic Area. Many visitors see only the "snow," but those who take time to really examine this exquisite flower are rewarded by the rare beauty depicted in the accompanying close-up picture. ❧

Bedstraw
Galium aparine   Madder family

These quite common plants are likely to be discussed on any spring guided hike. Their fascination arises from the way they stick to your clothing like the hooked portion of the popular zipperless closures. Legend has it that the plant was once used to stuff mattresses. There are several members of this genus in the Park. This particular one is common throughout the Park at low to mid elevations and blooms in April and May. They range from 8 to 40 inches in height with leaves ¾ to 1¾ inches long. This plant is also known as CLEAVERS. ❧

Birdfoot Violet
Viola pedata var. lineariloba   Violet family

This is one of many violets in the Great Smokies. Unlike the original birdfoot violet (*V. pedata var. pedata*) that has 2 dark and 3 lighter petals, all 5 petals of this variety are bluish-purple. It blooms from March through June, and is identified by the leaves, which somewhat resemble the shape of a bird's foot. A favorite habitat for this violet is the dry, open woods, especially along Park trails and roads, such as the Rich Mountain Road, between 900 and 3,000 feet elevation. ❧

White Fringed Phacelia   *W. Hutson photo*   *inset R. Hutson photo*

Bedstraw   *R. Hutson photo*

Birdfoot Violet   *R. Hutson photo*

Longspurred Violet
Viola rostrata   Violet family

This distinctively shaped violet with a long, slender spur is usually blue but sometimes white. Found on moist, wooded slopes at elevations of 1,000 to 3,500 feet, it blooms through April and May. The longspurred violet is closely related to dog violet (*V. conspersa*), the latter having bearded lateral petals and a shorter spur (less than 1/4"). Neither species is common in the Smokies, but the former may be found along the road to Greenbrier and in the Cosby area. ❧

Trout Lily
Erythronium americanum   Lily family

Few plants have such a widely accepted incorrect name, often being called DOG-TOOTH VIOLET although a lily and not a violet. The mottling of the 6 to 8-inch leaves suggests the speckled trout of the mountain streams. Other common names include ADDER'S TONGUE and FAWN LILY. Trout lily is widely distributed at lower elevations, but is sometimes found as high as 6,000 feet. The flowers, which appear in April and May, grow on stems 6 to 8 inches tall. Cherokee Indians regarded the flowering season of this lily as the time to fish for trout. It is found along the Cove Hardwood Nature Trail. ❧

Purple Phacelia
Phacelia bipinnatifida   Waterleaf family

Reaching a height of 12 to 24 inches, this is the tallest of the four phacelias in the Smokies. Purple phacelia blooms in April and May. It is found in some abundance at the start of the Chestnut Top Trail and along Park roads and trails from the valleys up to 2,000 feet elevation. ❧

Meadow Parsnip
Thaspium spp.   Parsley family

These common plants bloom in April though May at low to mid elevations. They stand up to 40 inches tall, with yellow infloresences (flower clusters) which are quite striking. There are several plants in the meadow parsnip (*Thaspium*) and golden alexander (*Zizia*) genera that require close examination in order to identify them. They can be separated at the generic level on the basis that the central flower of the golden alexander infloresence is sessile (has no flower stalk) whereas all the flowers in the meadow parsnip infloresence have a flower stalk. The golden alexanders are all yellow where as the meadow parsnips you are likely to encounter in the Park can be yellow or purple. ❧

Longspurred Violet *R. Hutson photo*

Trout Lily *R. Hutson photo*

Purple Phacelia *R. Hutson photo*

Meadow Parsnip *W. Hutson photo*

Flowering Dogwood
Cornus florida   Dogwood family

This popular small tree, found at elevations up to 3,500 feet, is noted for its profusion of blooms, its rich foliage, and its bright red fruits. The actual flowers are small, green, and centrally located. They are surrounded by showy white bracts that most laymen erroneously think are the petals. The foliage, dark green in summer and rich red in autumn, almost exceeds the beauty of the flowering tree. Flowers appear in April and May, with fruits maturing in September, and the leaves coloring in October. Two other species occur in the Park (alternate leaved dogwood, *C. alternifolia* p. 42, and silky dogwood, *C. amomum*). Flowering dogwood is the North Carolina State Flower. It may be found "almost anywhere" below 3,000 feet. This may change as an imported fungus is attacking and killing many of these trees. ❧

Redbud
Cercis canadensis   Pulse family

In early spring the deep pink flowers of the redbud do much to brighten the landscape up to about 1,500 feet elevation. The tree is unusual in that the flowers, which come in April and May, often appear directly from the trunk, as well as from the branches. JUDAS TREE is another common name, because it is said that Judas hanged himself from a redbud tree. Exceptionally fine displays of redbud may be seen in Little River Gorge. ❧

Silverbell
Halesia carolina   Storax family

Small white, bell-shaped flowers hang from the branches of this generally small to medium-sized tree which reaches large sizes here in the Park including the three current national co-champions (96, 103, and 104 feet tall). Many times, the fallen petals on the ground will alert you to its presence. It is abundant in rich, loamy, shaded soils from 900 to 5,000 feet elevation in the Smokies. Excellent displays may be seen in April and May along the Newfound Gap Road (U.S. 441) on both sides of the mountain and the Little River Road between Sugarlands and Elkmont. This sign of spring was also known locally as HEAVEN ABOVE. PEAWOOD is another common name. ❧

Flowering Dogwood

R. Hutson photo left, W. Hutson photo right

Redbud

W. Hutson photo

Silverbell

W. Hutson photo

Bishop's Cap
Mitella diphylla   Saxifrage family

T he creamy white flowers, appearing as tiny fringed bells when
  viewed under a magnifying lens, cling closely to the upper half
of the 10 to 15 inch stems. They appear in April and May at elevations up to 2,500 feet and may be seen in a large number of places
including the Bud Ogle and Sugarlands Nature Trails and the
Little River Gorge. The favorite habitat is moist, rich wooded slopes
and stream banks. MITERWORT is another common name. ❧

Foamflower
Tiarella cordifolia   Saxifrage family

T he white to creamy-white flowers, on stems 8 to 10 inches tall,
  appear in April and May. They are rather common on rich,
wooded slopes up to about 4,000 feet elevation and may be seen in
many places including along the Sugarlands Nature Trail, Cosby
Nature Trail and near Deep Creek Campground. ❧

Brook Lettuce
Saxifraga micranthidifolia   Saxifrage family

S omewhat similar to the Michaux's saxifrage (page 110), the
  leaves however do not have the same coarse tooth along the
edge. The typical brook lettuce plant is usually larger standing 12
to 30 inches tall. It is more common at low to mid elevations and
the Michaux's saxifrage higher up. Both are usually on moist, often
seeping rocks or stream beds. Brook lettuce blooms in April
through June. Another common name is MOUNTAIN LETTUCE ❧

Large-flowered Bellwort
Uvularia grandiflora   Lily family

T his plant, which stands 20 to 30 inches tall, is a cousin of wild
  oats (p. 46). It can be distinguished from wild and mountain
oats since their leaves clasp the stem where as the leaves of this
plant are seemingly pierced by the stem. Large-flowered bellwort is
more difficult to separate from perfoliate bellwort (*U. perfoliata*)
which has leaves with a smooth rather than a downy underside.
Large-flowered bellwort is found in wet areas at low to mid elevations in April and May. It can be found on the Ash Hopper Branch
Trail. ❧

Bishop's Cap *R. Hutson photo*

Foamflower *R. Hutson photo*

Brook Lettuce *W. Hutson photo*

Large-flowered Bellwort
R. Hutson photo

Yellow Trillium
Trillium luteum   Lily family

Three leaves, three petals, and three sepals characterize the trillium genus. This lemon-scented species, growing to a height of 8 to 12 inches, is a prominent spring flower up to an elevation of about 3,000 feet in the Smokies. It may be seen on the Cove Hardwood and Smokemont Nature Trails, where it blooms in April and May. A closely related species, Huger's trillium, has brownish-purple petals and a slightly unpleasant odor. ❧

Large-flowered Trillium
Trillium grandiflorum   Lily family

Perhaps the most abundant of the *Trilliums* of the Great Smokies, this is also one of the most beautiful. The big, bell-shaped white flower, which usually turns to a delicate pink with age, is on a stem 10 to 15 inches high and appears in April and May. The habitat is wooded slopes from 1,000 to 3,500 feet elevation. Considerable quantities grow in the vicinity of Chimneys Picnic Area. A common name used by the mountaineers for this *Trillium* was SNOW TRILLIUM because, as normally the first *Trillium* to bloom, it was presumably caught in late snowfalls from time to time. The yellow center of this *Trillium* helps distinguish it from the erect white variety of *T. erectum* (described below), which has a dark, and occasionally white, center. ❧

White Erect Trillium
Trillium erectum forma albiflorum   Lily family

This common lovely white trillium, reaching a height of 10 to 12 inches, blooms in April and May. This *Trillium* has a generally dark center which helps to distinguish it from *T. grandiflorum* (described above). It is found from the foothills up to 5,500 feet in elevation. There is a fine display at the upper end of the tunnel on the road to Cades Cove. This is the white form of purple wakerobin (p. 74) hence another common name WHITE WAKEROBIN. ❧

Yellow Trillium

W. Hutson photo

**Large-flowered
Trillium**

W. Hutson photo

**White Erect
Trillium**

R. Hutson photo

Stonecrop
Sedum ternatum   Orpine family

The small white flowers, on fleshy plants from 4 to 5 inches tall and with whorled, ovate leaves, appear in April and May. Its preferred habitat is moss-covered boulders and bluffs and stream banks at elevations up to 2,500 feet. It may be seen along the Huskey Gap Trail and in Little River Gorge. The genus name, *Sedum*, is also used as a common name by many people. This is the only native *Sedum* in the Smokies. There are four introduced species, *S. acre, S. sarmentosum, S. spectabile,* and *S. telephium* all of which are fortunately rare within the Park. ❧

Crested Dwarf Iris
Iris cristata   Iris family

Widely distributed at lower elevations of the Smokies, this beautiful iris does much to brighten the roadsides during April and May. The flower is usually a rich blue, but occasionally a light purple or even white. It is 4 to 6 inches tall and is found mostly on open slopes. Spring dwarf iris (*I. verna var. smalliana*) and southern blue flag (*I. virginica*) are the only other native species of this genius within the Park and neither are common here. They can be separated on the basis that southern blue flag is the only one with a flowering stem more than 6 inches tall and crested dwarf iris has crested sepals whereas spring dwarf iris does not. Iris is the Tennessee State Flower. Look for the crested dwarf iris in Little River Gorge, Bud Ogle Nature Trail, and Porters Creek Trail. ❧

Spicebush
Lindera benzoin   Laurel family

This shrub is easily identified by the pleasant spicy odor of crushed leaves, young stems or fruits. The yellow flowers are unisexual but often both sexes occur on the same plant. It produces small, ovate red fruits. Spicebush flowers in March and April and rarely early fall. The plant is found on moist alluvial soils at lower elevations such as along the Ash Hopper Branch trail. Often it is associated with old homesites as mountaineers used the plant to make a tea. The only other member of this family occurring in the Park is sassafras (*Sassafras albidum*). ❧

26

Stonecrop

W. Hutson photo

**Crested Dwarf
Iris**

R. Hutson photo

Spicebush

R. Hutson photo

Wood Anemone
Anemone lancifolia   Buttercup family

The flower has no petals, but the white, petal-like sepals, occasionally tinged with pink, appear in April and May on plants up to 8 inches tall. Fairly common up to 3,000 feet elevation, it may be seen in moist, woodsy soil along the Abrams Falls Trail. This plant which is also known as MOUNTAIN or LANCED LEAVED WOOD ANEMONE sometimes intergrades with *A. quinquefolia* which has 5 (quinque meaning five) leaflets or 3 leaflets with the lateral leaflets having sharp deep cuts. ❧

Creeping Phlox
Phlox stolonifera   Phlox family

Sizable spots of bright color ranging from blue to pink-purple, seen along Park roads in April and May, are likely to be creeping phlox. It is 8 to 10 inches tall and is found along the Little River Road and elsewhere from 1,000 to 3,500 feet elevation. The creeping is done by stolons; hence the species name. ❧

Wild Geranium
Geranium maculatum   Geranium family

Pink to purple flowers appear in April and May on stems 12 to 18 inches tall. Because of its long, slender fruits, this geranium is sometimes called CRANESBILL. It distributes its seeds by literally hurling them into the air when this pod bursts. It is fairly common on wooded slopes up to 3,500 feet, such as along Sugarlands and Bud Ogle Nature Trails and near Deep Creek Campground. The other native *Geranium* in the Park is Carolina cranesbill, *G. carolinianum,* which has smaller petals (less than a ½ inch long). ❧

Wood Anemone

W. Hutson photo

Creeping Phlox

W. Hutson photo

Wild Geranium

W. Hutson photo

Princess Tree
Paulownia tomentosa   Figwort family

Native to Asia, this fast-growing tree apparently is well established in the Smokies at elevations up to 2,500 feet. Known locally as EMPRESS TREE, the flowers appear in late April and early May before the opposite leaves, which resemble the whorled *Catalpa* leaves. The Japanese prize the wood above all others, using it to make watertight boxes for storing valuable possessions. Traditionally the tree was often planted at a daughter's birth, for her dowry. ❧

Striped Maple
Acer pensylvanicum   Maple family

One of 7 maples in the Smokies, this tree, usually less than 35 feet tall, has green bark, striped with white, and light green flowers. Found from 1,000 to 3,500 feet elevation, it flowers on Elkmont Nature Trail in late April and May. In addition to the striped bark (hence the name striped maple), the leaf is very distinctive having the shape of a goose's webbed footprint. Other common names include PENNSYLVANIA MAPLE, MOOSEWOOD, and GOOSE-FOOT MAPLE. ❧

Lyre-leaved Sage
Salvia lyrata   Mint family

Lyre-leaved sage derives its name from the rosette of lyre shaped leaves at the base of this 12 to 24 inch tall plant. Occasionally there are an additional one or two pairs of smaller leaves on the stem. The angularity of the stem is a trademark of members of the mint family. The flowers, which appear in April and May, are violet or blue, rarely white. It is frequently found along roadsides throughout the Park at low to mid elevations and in some areas occurring even at higher elevations such as Mile High. ❧

Robin's-plantain
Erigeron pulchellus   Composite family

Robin's-plantain is a 6 to 20 inch tall perennial herb whose branching is limited to the flower head bearing part of the stem. The plant has a beautiful rosette of basal leaves with a few small leaves on the stem above. The flowering head is composed of a center cluster of yellow flowers surrounded by a rim of lavender to white ray flowers. One of the earliest blooming composites, it is common in April to June at the lower elevations. ❧

30

Princess Tree *W. Hutson photo*

Striped Maple *W. Hutson photo*

Lyre-leaved Sage *R. Hutson photo*

Robin's-plantain *R. Hutson photo*

Wild Strawberry
Fragaria virginiana   Rose family

The white flowers appear in April and May on plants 6-7 inches tall, which spread by runners and have "three-fingered" leaves. Its appearance is reminiscent of common cinquefoil (p. 58). Delicious red fruits start maturing in June along roads and trailsides at lower elevations, such as near Fightin' Creek Gap, and as late as August at higher levels, as on Parson Bald (4,700 feet). ❧

Yellow Mandarin
Disporum lanuginosum   Lily family

Usually a pair of bell shaped yellow flowers, each with free sepals and petals about 3/4 of an inch in length, are borne at the end of the branches in April and May. The smooth red berries are quite striking. It differs from the similar twisted stalks (*Streptopus,* p. 80) where the flowers are borne along the branch in the axil of the leaves. Although it can grow to a height of 30 inches, most plants are considerably shorter. Yellow mandarin grows at low to mid elevations and can be found on the Cove Hardwood Nature Trail. ❧

Common Blue Violet
Viola papilionacea   Violet family

This is one of the very common blue violets flowering usually in spring, but occasionally, later in the season. Occurring at low to mid elevations, the plant has no stem the leaves and flowers attaching directly to a slender root stock. Violets hybridize freely and it is difficult to identify them with certainty. The plant with five leaflets is a common cinquefoil (p. 58). ❧

Wild Strawberry

R. Hutson photo

**Yellow
Mandarin**

R. Hutson photo
W. Hutson photo inset

**Common Blue
Violet**

W. Hutson photo

False Solomon's-seal
Smilacina racemosa   Lily family

The terminal flower cluster easily distinguishes this species from the true Solomon's-seal. Growing in areas below 3,500 feet, it is plentiful in Little River Gorge where the plume-like flowers appear from late April to June. The stems are 15 to 25 inches in height. Other common names include SOLOMON'S PLUME, SOLOMON'S ZIGZAG, and FALSE SPIKENARD. ❧

Solomon's-seal
Polygonatum biflorum   Lily family

This gracefully arching herb, usually 2 to 3 feet long, has greenish-yellow, axillary flowers which appear in April and May. It grows on moist slopes below 3,000 feet elevation, occurring abundantly in Little River Gorge and along most of the nature trails. Also known as SMOOTH SOLOMON'S SEAL, it can be differentiated from hairy solomon's-seal (*P. pubescens*) which has hairs on the underside of its leaf particularly on the veins. Great solomon's-seal (*P. canaliculatum*) is a larger version of *P. biflorum* and many consider it simply a larger plant, not a separate species. ❧

Rue Anemone
Thalictrum (Anemonella) thalictroides   Buttercup family

The delicate white flowers, on plants 6 to 8 inches tall, appear in April and May on wooded slopes up to 3,000 feet. Fairly abundant, they may be found along the Rich Mountain Road and along the Cove Hardwood Nature Trail. The species is often confused with wood anemone (p. 28), which has fewer and larger sepals. Neither has true petals, the sepals being petal-like. Looking beyond the flower, the leaf of rue anemone, upon close examination, is also quite distinctive. ❧

False Solomon's-seal

W. Hutson photo

Solomon's-seal

W. Hutson photo

Rue Anemone

W. Hutson photo

Gay Wings
Polygala paucifolia   Milkwort family

Only 3 to 4 inches tall, this perennial herb is rare in the Smokies. It has been found along the trail to Abrams Falls. The attractive orchid-pink flowers are seen in April. It is also known as FLOWERING WINTERGREEN, FRINGED POLYGALA and BIRD-ON-THE-WING. ❧

Great Chickweed
Stellaria pubera   Pink family

Five white petals, often mistaken for ten petals because each petal is so deeply cleft, give a star-like appearance to this wildflower. For this reason it is also known as STAR CHICKWEED. A close look reveals tiny black balls or anthers at the tips of the stamens. The flowers appear in April and May, on stems 6 to 8 inches tall. Common on wooded slopes and roadsides up to 4,000 feet elevation, the plant is found along Smokemont and Cove Hardwood Nature Trails. ❧

Jack-in-the-pulpit
Arisaema triphyllum   Arum family

Easily recognized either by the unique "Jack" standing erect in his pulpit or by the one or two three-part leaves, this common plant is widely distributed in the lower Park elevations. From April to June it is found along Smokemont Nature Trail, at the start of Huskey Gap Trail and most other trails particularly at the lower elevations. At the base of the "Jack" is a cluster of tiny flowers; a green or dark purple spathe forms the pulpit and curves over to provide a canopy. The red fruit is quite striking. Another name is INDIAN TURNIP. ❧

Gay Wings

W. Hutson photo

**Great
Chickweed**

W. Hutson photo

Jack-in-the-pulpit

W. Hutson photo
R. Hutson photo far right

North American Pawpaw
Asimina triloba   Custard-apple family

The slightly reddish chocolate-brown flowers appear in April on trees up to 20 feet high. The edible fruits mature in August and September. Somewhat uncommon, the tree is found only in a few moist locations up to 2,500 feet. One thicket occurs between Gatlinburg and Park headquarters and another above Smokemont. This is the Park's only member of an important family of tropical fruits. ❧

Halberd-leaved Violet
Viola hastata   Violet family

The variegated leaf blade resembling an arrow point character- izes this species making it easy to identify even without its yel- low flowers. Growing 4 to 10 inches tall, it is usually found at low to mid elevations throughout in spring as for example along the Bud Ogle Nature Trail. ❧

Canada Violet
Viola canadensis   Violet family

Canada violet is the tallest of the Park's approximately 26 species, with a stem from 10 to 12 inches tall. Its white flowers, darken- ing later to a pale blue or light purple, are seen from April to June at elevations up to 4,000 feet. It is widely distributed on rich, wooded slopes, and may be found in abundance along the Cove Hardwood Nature Trail. ❧

North American Pawpaw

W. Hutson photo

Halberd-leaved Violet

R. Hutson photo

Canada Violet

W. Hutson photo

Painted Trillium
Trillium undulatum   Lily family

Oone of the approximately 9 trilliums of the Great Smokies, the painted trillium is found on moist, shaded slopes from 3,000 to 6,500 feet elevation. It reaches a height of 8 to 12 inches, and blooms in April and May. The "painted" part of the name refers to the pink "V" at the base of the white petals. It may be seen on Mt. Le Conte and Clingmans Dome. ❦

Toothwort
Dentaria diphylla   Mustard family

The white to pink or purple flowers, on stems from 8 to 10 inches tall, appear in April and May. Fairly common along Park trails and roads and on rich wooded slopes at elevations up to 3,500 feet, toothwort is easily found in Little River Gorge and elsewhere. Also known as PEPPERROOT because of the acrid rootstock, this is one of the wild "salads" called creases or cresses by mountain people. The other common toothwort in the park (cut-leaved toothwort, *D. laciniata*) can generally be distinguished by its three whorled stem leaves which are deeply divided into narrow segments versus two nearly opposite stem leaves for *diphylla* which are divided into three broad leaflets. Another common name for cut-leaf toothwort is crowsfoot due to the shape of the divided leaves. ❦

Black Locust
Robinia pseudoacacia   Pulse family

Loaded with clusters of white flowers, these plentiful trees make an attractive display on the mountainsides below 3,000 feet elevation in April and May. They are especially noticeable in the Sugarlands between Park Headquarters and Chimney Tops and along the Little River Road. Major blooms, unfortunately, do not occur most years. The wood is noted for its durability and was used for a variety of things by the pioneers and Cherokees. ❦

Dwarf Ginseng
Panax trifolius   Ginseng family

This dainty plant stands 4 to 8 inches tall with 3 whorled leaves which are divided into 3-5 leaflets. It is smaller than the only other member of this genus in the Park, ginseng (*P. quinquefolius*), which is tragically being heavily poached for use in Chinese and other herbal remedies. Blooming April though June at low to middle elevations, dwarf ginseng can be found on the Cosby Nature Trail and in the Sugarlands area. ❦

Painted Trillium *R. Hutson photo*

Toothwort *W. Hutson photo*

Black Locust *W. Hutson photo*

Dwarf Ginseng *R. Hutson photo*

Doll's-eyes
Actaea pachypoda   Buttercup family

T he interesting white fruits which mature in August and
  September get more attention than do the white flowers of late
April and May. Not abundant, the plant grows to 2 feet tall in scat-
tered locations up to 3,000 feet. It may be seen along the
Sugarlands Nature Trail and Porters Creek Trail. Another com-
mon name is WHITE BANEBERRY. ❧

Columbine
Aquilegia canadensis   Buttercup family

W ith strikingly beautiful flowers, the wild columbine presents
  an elegant show, as along the lower portion of Little River
Gorge and near the Bud Ogle Cabin. It is fairly common throughout April and early May. Abundant at elevations of 900 to 2,500
feet, the columbine also is seen occasionally at much higher elevations, such as at Mile High where it blooms in early summer.
Usually 18 to 24 inches high, the plant is especially attractive
against a background of a rock cliff or the foamy water of a nearby
stream. Because of the length of the flower, the hummingbird is a
preferred pollinator. ❧

Alternate-leaved Dogwood
Cornus alternifolia   Dogwood family

A lso known as PAGODA DOGWOOD (because of its peculiar branching) and GREEN OSIER, this small tree can be seen along the
Clingmans Dome Road. Showy clusters of white flowers, without
large bracts, are found in April and May at lower elevations but
appear somewhat later higher up. Fruits of this dogwood, which
ripen in August and September, are blue, in contrast to the bright
red ones of the flowering dogwood (p. 20). ❧

Doll's-eyes

W. Hutson photos

Columbine

W. Hutson photo

Alternate-leaved Dogwood

W. Hutson photo

Dutchman's-pipe
Aristolochia macrophylla (durior)   Birthwort family

This climbing vine gets its name from the similarity of the flower's shape to that of the traditional pipe of the Dutch. The large heart shaped leaves are very distinctive. It is fairly common in the moist woods of the Smokies up to about 4,000 feet, but the flowers which appear in April and May are seldom seen because of their greenish color and because so many of them bloom high in the trees. The species may be seen along the roadside from the Chimneys Picnic Area up to the Alum Cave Trailhead. ⚘

Carolina Vetch
Vicia caroliniana   Pulse family

This, the Park's only native *Vicia* is a common perennial herbaceous vine, up to 3 feet in length with slender clusters of small white, pea like flowers. It is often seen on trailsides and on road banks at low to mid elevations. The plant flowers in April and May. Another common name is WOOD VETCH. ⚘

Cross Vine
Bignonia capreolata   Bignonia family

These golden-yellow, trumpet-shaped flowers with red centers are found from 1,000 to 2,500 feet elevation, in late April to early May, especially in Little River Gorge, along the Gatlinburg Trail and at the start of the Chestnut Top Trail. The tall, slender vines climb rock cliffs and trees alike, with flowers often seen 30 to 50 feet above ground. It is a representative of a large tropical family. ⚘

Lousewort
Pedicularis canadensis   Figwort family

If you find the name "lousewort" to be somewhat offensive, you may call it WOOD-BETONY. People once believed that cattle would become infested with lice upon touching this plant. The pale yellow to reddish-brown flowers appear in April and May on stems 8 to 12 inches tall. The leaves are fern-like. It occurs up to 3,500 feet elevation and may be seen along the Roaring Fork Motor Nature Trail and the Blue Ridge Parkway between Oconaluftee and the Heintooga Ridge Road turn off. The plant is often partially parasitic, being attached to roots of other plants. ⚘

Dutchman's-pipe   *R. Hutson photo*

Carolina Vetch   *R. Hutson photo*

Cross Vine   *W. Hutson photo*

Lousewort   *R. Hutson photo*

Witch-hobble
Viburnum lantanoides (alnifolium)   Honeysuckle family

Legend has it that this plant will keep witches away, hence the name. Although sometimes found at intermediate elevations, witch-hobble or HOBBLEBUSH is particularly abundant in the moist, rich, shaded soils of the spruce-fir forests. The large white, marginal flowers surrounding the smaller central blossoms make a fine display in late April and May. The bright red fruits and the beautifully colored leaves of late August through October are equally attractive. The plant is seen in many places along the crest of the Smokies and to good advantage along the Spruce-Fir Nature Trail. This shrub, growing to a height of 6 to 10 feet, is one of eight *Viburnum* species in the Park. ❧

Wild Oats
Uvularia sessilifolia   Lily family

Also known as SMALL BELLWORT, the yellow, drooping flower appears on a stem 8 to 10 inches tall. It is very similar to mountain bellwort *U. puberula (pudica)*. Although widely distributed through lower elevations of the Smokies, it is seldom found in large numbers at any location. Several plants may be seen in April and May along the Cades Cove Nature Trail and the Rich Mt. Road. ❧

Pinxter-flower
Rhododendron periclymenoides (nudiflorum)   Heath family

This shrub, also known as PURPLE HONEYSUCKLE, grows 4 to 8 feet tall. Because of the shape of its flowers, which open from mid-April to mid-May, it often is confused with honeysuckle. Pinxter-flower is widely scattered, but not rare, in open woodlands at lower Park elevations, and may be seen in the Abrams Creek area and along the Foothills Parkway in the vicinity of Look Rock. ❧

Witch-hobble

R. Hutson photo

Wild Oats

W. Hutson photo

Pinxter-flower

W. Hutson photo

Fringe Tree
Chionanthus virginicus   Olive family

F ringe tree is a small tree or tall to low shrub with oval to elliptic opposite leaves 4-8 inches in length. The flowers are borne in white fringe like clusters in April and May to be followed by black or dark blue berry like fruits. It has found acceptance with horticulturists as an ornamental. Within the Park, it is found on lower Abrams Creek and at the Sugarlands Visitor Center. ❧

Showy Orchis
Galearis (Orchis) spectabilis   Orchid family

W ith a combination of white and pink to lavender petals, this is regarded by many as the prettiest of the over 30 orchids of the Great Smokies. It is rather rare, usually occurring as only two or three clusters of four or five plants each. Occasionally, however, there will be a score or more such clusters in a radius of 100 feet. The flowers, on stems 6 to 8 inches tall, appear in April and May in moist, wooded areas with loamy soil at elevations of 1,500 to 3,000 feet. Showy Orchis may be seen along the Bud Ogle and Cosby Nature Trails. ❧

Umbrella Magnolia
Magnolia tripetala   Magnolia family

T his is one of the three magnolias native to the Smokies that you are likely to encounter. All are deciduous. This species gets its name from the umbrella-like arrangement of the long leaves. The cream-white flowers, which appear in April and May, are the Park's largest flowers, some petals being 10 to 12 inches long. *M. tripetala* grows along the Bud Ogle Nature Trail and in Little River Gorge. The other two common species are cucumber tree or magnolia (*M. acuminata*) and fraser magnolia (*M. fraseri*). The way the leaves are shaped at their base identifies the species. Umbrella magnolia forms a "V", fraser a "W" and cucumber a "U". All three species are fairly common up to about 4,000 feet elevation. Both the national co-champion fraser magnolias (110 and 107 feet tall) lie within the Park. A fourth native magnolia, big leaf magnolia (*M. macrophylla*), is found at low elevations and is rare within the Park. It's leaf too forms a "W" shape at it's base but generally exceed 18" in overall length and has hairs on it's underside. ❧

48

Fringe Tree

R. Hutson photo

Showy Orchis

W. Hutson photo

**Umbrella
Magnolia**

W. Hutson photo

Umbrella-leaf
Diphylleia cymosa   Barberry family

Related to May-apple (p. 56), this perennial herb is occasionally more than 24 inches tall. The relatively small white flowers appear above the leaves in April and May. Umbrella-leaf is also quite beautiful when the fruit ripens and it's leaves change color. Its favorite habitat is very wet, rocky slopes or seeps, usually in deep shade, at elevations from 2,500 to 6,000 feet. Rather rare and restricted to the Southern Appalachians, umbrella-leaf may be found on the Balsam Mountain Road and alongside the highway above the Chimney Tops Trailhead. An almost identical sister species occurs in the Alps of Japan. ❧

Daisy Fleabane
Erigeron philadelphicus   Composite family

With its head of yellow disc flowers surrounded by white (rarely pink) ray flowers, this plant resembles a miniature daisy. Eighteen to 30 inches tall, daisy fleabane is quite common at elevations from 1,000 to 2,500 feet. It may be seen along the Little River Gorge Road below Elkmont, where it flowers from April through August. The plant was once used to repel fleas. Other names for this plant are PHILADELPHIA or COMMON FLEABANE. A closely related spring species is robin's-plantain (p. 30), which has larger heads. ❧

Fire Cherry
Prunus pensylvanica   Rose family

Fire cherry is a normally small, shiny, barked tree with slender leaves and clusters of white flowers borne from a single point. It usually follows fire, hence the common name, or a cut over area, but persists in the new forest as it develops. They grow to a large size in the Park which is home to one of the national co-champions (85 feet tall). It flowers in April and May from the mid-elevations on up and can be seen along the Newfound Gap Road. This tree is also known as PIN CHERRY. ❧

50

Umbrella-leaf

R. Hutson photo
W. Hutson photo inset

Daisy Fleabane

W. Hutson photo

Fire Cherry

R. Hutson photo

Star Grass
Hypoxis hirsuta   Amaryllis family

Except for the difference in leaf arrangement and flower color, this small plant somewhat resembles blue-eyed grass (p. 80) and belongs to a closely related plant family. Leaves are in two rows in blue-eyed grass and in spirals in star grass. The latter may be found along the Laurel Falls Trail and roadsides at mid to low elevations in late April and May. ❧

Whorled Pogonia
Isotria verticillata   Orchid family

This interesting but extremely rare orchid, also known as FIVE-LEAVED ORCHID, is found in only a few scattered pine-oak forests in the Smokies. The plant, reaching a height of 8 to 16 inches, sometimes grows near pink lady's-slipper. It is seen in April and May. Because of it's scarcity, we do not disclose its location or that of other rare plants. ❧

Blue Cohosh
Caulophyllum thalictroides   Barberry family

The yellowish-green flowers, on plants about 2 feet tall, appear in late April and May. Fairly common in rich woodlands up to about 3,000 feet elevation, they may be seen on the Cove Hardwood Nature Trail. An unusual feature is that the fast-growing seed ruptures its green fruit-covering, which remains below the blue, spherical seed at maturity. Other common names are ELECTRIC LIGHT BULB PLANT and PAPOOSE-ROOT. This plant is not related to the black cohosh (p. 94), also common in the Smokies. ❧

Beard-tongue
Penstemon canescens   Figwort family

Clusters of light lavender or purple-striped flowers on plants 12 to 18 inches tall, make attractive displays along Park roads from April to July. It is also known as HAIRY BEARD-TONGUE. Look for them in Cades Cove. Another species occurs at Mile High. The common name refers to a bearded, sterile stamen that appears in each flower. ❧

Star Grass *W. Hutson photo*

Whorled Pogonia *Heilman photo*

Blue Cohosh *R. Hutson photo*

Beard-tongue *W. Hutson photo*

Yellow Lady's-slipper
Cypripedium calceolus var. pubescens   Orchid family

With its yellow "moccasin" and slightly curled brown sepals, this orchid has a scattered distribution in the Smokies. Growing on moist, rich slopes from 900 to 3,000 feet, it reaches a height of 12 to 18 inches. It blooms in May. If the pouch is less than 1 inch long, it is the small yellow lady's-slipper (*var. parviflorum*). A relative, the pink lady's-slipper (p. 56), is locally more abundant but still rare. These species are also known as MOCCASIN FLOWER. ❧

Fairy-wand
Chamaelirium luteum   Lily family

Although it occurs in small, scattered colonies in several sections of the Smokies up to 2,500 feet elevation, this lily is rather uncommon. It grows along the Cades Cove Road, where it flowers in May and June. The white, curved flower-spikes appear at the top of stems 15 to 24 inches long. Male and female flowers occur on separate plants. The one shown here is a male. The plant is also known as BLAZING STAR, RATTLESNAKE ROOT and DEVILS-BIT. ❧

Wild Ginger
Asarum canadense var. acuminatum   Birthwort family

The heart-shaped leaves of this ginger species last only one season in contrast to the evergreen leaves of little brown jugs (below). The meaty, jug-like flowers have three long, slender, flaring sepals but no petals. It is fairly abundant on rich slopes along streams at elevations up to 3,000 feet. The unusual brown flowers appearing in April and May may be seen on the Cove Hardwood Nature Trail and Little River Trail. It is a variety of *A. canadense*, which typically has shorter sepals with more rounded tips. ❧

Little Brown Jug
Hexastylis arifolia (Asarum arifolium)   Birthwort family

Its arrow-shaped leaves and fleshy jug-shaped calyx—a flower without petals—give this plant a unique appeal. The thick, evergreen leaves are a familiar sight on wooded slopes up to 3,000 feet. Often hidden by the leaves, the interesting jugs occur at ground level, in May, and are purplish-brown and less than an inch long. Look for them along Sugarlands Nature Trail and Porters Creek Trail. Mountain children often pressed the fragrant leaves in their schoolbooks. Other names include PIGS PLANT, WILD GINGER, and HEART-LEAF. ❧

Yellow Lady's-slipper   *W. Hutson photo*

Fairy-wand   *R. Hutson photo*

Wild Ginger   *W. Hutson photo*

Little Brown Jug   *R. Hutson photo*

Squaw-root
Conopholis americana   Broom-rape family

This parasite, growing on oak roots, is also known as CANCER-ROOT and SQUAW-CORN. Ranging in height from 4 to 9 inches, the brown-colored plant, without chlorophyll, resembles a slender pine cone or a small ear of corn. It is rather uncommon, although widely distributed in oak forests below 4,500 feet elevation. Squaw-root may be seen in late April and May along the Laurel Falls Trail and Rich Mountain Road. ❧

Pink Lady's-slipper
Cypripedium acaule   Orchid family

Generally rare, this orchid is locally abundant in a few Great Smokies' locations below 3,000 feet. The stately pink flower with curled brown sepals appears at the top of a leafless stalk 12 to 18 inches in height. It is also known as PINK MOCCASIN FLOWER and may be seen in April and May. Lady's-slippers form a symbiotic relationship with a fungus that is crucial for their survival. Poaching, a major problem for lady's-slippers, is made all the more tragic as they rarely survive transplanting. Combined with a low reproduction rate, their future seems bleak. ❧

May-apple
Podophyllum peltatum   Barberry family

Also known as MANDRAKE, this plant is 10 to 18 inches tall and has two prominent leaves whose stalks attach to their undersides within the leaf margin. A single inconspicuous flower appears in May near the junction of the leaf stalks. Colonies of 50 to 100 or more plants grow in open woods and on road shoulders up to 2,500 feet and are easily recognized along the Cove Hardwood Nature Trail and Cades Cove Loop Road. ❧

Squaw-root

W. Hutson photo

Pink Lady's-slipper

W. Hutson photo

May-apple

W. Hutson photo

Common Cinquefoil
Potentilla canadensis   Rose family

A lso known as FIVE-FINGERS and DWARF CINQUEFOIL referring to the number of leaflets, this yellow-flowered plant resembles wild strawberry (p. 32) except for flower color and number of leaflets. Flowers appear in May and June, followed by inconspicuous dry fruits. They may be seen, along with wild strawberries, on road shoulders near Fightin' Creek Gap. ❧

Pipsissewa
Chimaphila maculata   Wintergreen family

T his small evergreen shrub, 6 to 9 inches tall, is widely scattered in dry, acid woodlands up to 4,000 feet elevation and may be observed along the Cosby and Sugarlands Nature Trails. From one to three pendant flowers to a stem appear in May and June. Although the plant is also known as SPOTTED WINTERGREEN, its leaves have stripes rather than spots. The common name STRIPPED WINTERGREEN, would seem more appropriate. ❧

Vasey's Trillium
Trillium vaseyi   Lily family

T his *Trillium* has the largest flower of all species, often nearly 4 inches in diameter. The dark maroon-purple flowers hanging below the leaves appear on plants up to 30 inches tall from May to early July. Although limited to the Southern Appalachians and generally rare in the Smokies, it is locally rather abundant in a few moist, deep-shaded locations below 3,500 feet, such as between Cherokee Orchard and Rainbow Falls and the Cosby Nature Trail. ❧

Catesby's Trillium
Trillium catesbaei   Lily family

T he white pendant flowers, on stems 10 to 12 inches tall, appear in May. Some petals turn pink with age, but a few are pink from the first. Although a rare species, limited to the Southern Appalachians, several plants may be seen along the Cades Cove Nature Trail, Abrams Falls Trail, and Schoolhouse Gap Trail. Unlike most wildflowers, it takes six years for a *Trillium* to flower. ❧

Common Cinquefoil *R. Hutson photo*

Pipsissewa *R. Hutson photo*

Vasey's Trillium *W. Hutson photo*

Catesby's Trillium *R. Hutson photo*

Indian Cucumber Root
Medeola virginiana   Lily family

The upper whorl of three leaves and the lower whorl of 6 to 10 larger leaves are hallmarks of this dainty 8 to 32 inch tall plant. The greenish yellow flowers hang below the upper whorl. These upper leaves in fall become streaked with red at their base and, although the flowers hung limply below the leaves, the flower stalk stiffens and straightens as the beautiful black berries ripen holding them above the red streaked upper leaves as if to say to wildlife, "come and get me". It can be seen in May and June along the Cosby Nature Trail, Grotto Falls Trail, and throughout the Park although more common at the lower to mid elevations. ❧

Mountain Laurel
Kalmia latifolia   Heath family

Laurel, a shrub which occasionally reaches the size of a small tree, thrives at elevations up to 5,000 feet and occasionally occurs as high as 6,000 feet. It blooms in May on the lower slopes but from mid-June to July at the high elevations. A good way to distinguish laurel and rhododendron when not in flower is: "short leaf, short name; long leaf, long name." Early settlers knew laurel as ivy, and rhododendron as laurel. ❧

Bleeding Heart
Dicentra eximia   Fumitory family

This beautiful wildflower, rare in the Smokies, grows approximately 12 inches tall. Its habitat is moist bluffs along stream banks at elevations of 1,000 to 2,500 feet, particularly along Little River Gorge. Its flower is a pink version of the related squirrel corn (p. 12) and its foliage is similar but bleeding heart is taller. It blooms in May. ❧

Indian
Cucumber Root

R. Hutson photos

Mountain
Laurel

R. Hutson photo

Bleeding Heart

W. Hutson photo

Golden Ragwort
Senecio aureus   Composite family

The conspicuous yellow flower-heads, on plants 15 to 25 inches tall, are common from April through July in moist soil below 2,500 feet in the Park and along roads in the surrounding region. In early spring, the leaves are quite an attraction. ❧

Bristly Locust
Robinia hispida   Pulse family

This 5 to 6 foot tall shrub with beautiful pink flowers occurs at lower to mid-elevations. Hairs may be dense or scarce on stems and leaves. It is most abundant along roadsides or open woods and usually flowers in May. ❧

Fire Pink
Silene virginica   Pink family

The scarlet fire pink, about a foot tall, is usually found on dry, steep banks along roads and trails at elevations of 1,500 to 2,500 feet. It is seen in April at the lower elevations, but as late as May and June at higher levels. Little River Gorge is a good place to look for fire pink, which is a relative of starry campion (*S. stellata*, p.122) and five other *Silene* species in the Smokies. ❧

Putty Root
Aplectum hyemale   Orchid family

This inconspicuous plant is sometimes called ADAM AND EVE orchid. The variously colored (greenish, yellowish, brownish, or whitish) flowers with purplish markings bloom in the spring, but the single over wintering basal leaf does not appear until fall. Because it lacks a leaf at flowering time, many people think it is leafless. It also gave rise to the local name RESURRECTION ORCHID since the flower appeared after the death of the leaf in spring. Ramp (p. 108) and crane-fly orchid (p. 122) are similarly leafless when they bloom. Putty root can be found in rich moist woods at low to mid elevations in May and June. ❧

62

Golden Ragwort   *W. Hutson photo*

Bristly Locust
R. Hutson photo

Fire Pink   *R. Hutson photo*

Putty Root   *R. Hutson photo*

Mountain Maple
Acer spicatum   Maple family

Fairly common on moist, wooded slopes at elevations from 3,000 to 6,500 feet, this small tree with a shrubby appearance has erect, light green spikes of flowers and slightly wrinkled leaves. It may be seen along the road banks near Indian Gap from May into July. ❧

Dog-hobble
Leucothoë fontanesiana (editorum)   Heath family

This arching 5 to 7-foot shrub usually grows in dense thickets in moist, shaded, acid soils from 900 to 5,000 feet. Dog-hobble is restricted to the Southern Appalachians. The strongly scented white flowers hang in clusters and appear in May and June. Its deciduous relative, fetter bush (*L. recurva*), is the only other species in the Smokies. In pre-Park days, when bear hunting was practiced, the heavy bears could escape pursuing dogs by forcing their way through dense thickets of these shrubs, whereas the dogs became "hobbled" by the tangled growth. Look for this shrub along the Cosby Nature Trail or the Roaring Fork Motor Nature Trail. ❧

Serviceberry
Amelanchier laevis   Rose family

The slender, white to pale pink petals with brown sepals appear as early as March in the foothills, with the flowering season advancing progressively up the mountain slopes. At elevations of 5,000 to 6,000 feet, blooms are found in late May and June. Legend has it that the tree bloomed about the time when the circuit riding preachers got out to conduct the first services of the year in early spring hence the name serviceberry. Most mountain people call it SARVIS, the Old English pronunciation for "service," and the plant is also known as SHADBUSH. The dark-red fruits, which are edible, ripen from May to August, depending on elevation. Serviceberry is abundant in Little River Gorge and in the Mile High area. Both the national co-champions grow within the park (73 and 78 feet tall). ❧

Mountain Maple

W. Hutson photo

Dog-hobble

W. Hutson photo

Serviceberry

R. Hutson photo

Clinton's Lily
Clintonia umbellulata   Lily family

Two species of this rare lily, named for an early New York governor and conservationist, are found in the Smokies. This white-flowered one, also known as SPECKLED WOOD LILY, is found only in the Southern Appalachians. In the Smokies it blooms in May at 2,000 to 3,000 feet, as between Cherokee Orchard and Rainbow Falls. The shiny blue fruits are quite attractive in August and September. The other yellow flowered species (yellow bead lily, p. 68) blooms in June mostly at higher elevations, as along the Spruce-Fir Nature Trail. Both species are also called BEAD LILY. ⅜

Lily-leaved Twayblade
Liparis lilifolia   Orchid family

A rather small plant with two (hence the name twayblade tway meaning two) glossy basal (lily like) leaves. Several purplish flowers with greenish white sepals are borne on a 4 to 10 inch angled stalk or raceme in May and June. The plant is restricted to moist wooded or heavily shaded areas at low elevations such as the Elkmont Nature Trail. ⅜

Galax
Galax aphylla   Diapensia family

This plant is more widely known for the beauty of its leaves, which turn copper-red in winter, than for its stately white spikes of flowers. The flower stem, seen in May and June, reaches a height of 10 to 15 inches.It is abundant in dry woods up to 5,000 feet elevation, and may be seen along the Laurel Falls Trail. Galax is often called COLTSFOOT because of the shape of the leaves. ⅜

Waterleaf
Hydrophyllum virginianum   Waterleaf family
var. atranthum

This plant is a 12 to 24-inch tall perennial with dark violet flowers. The original waterleaf (*var. virginianum*) has lighter white to lavender flowers. Our variety grows throughout the Park in moist woods at mid to high elevations and blooms in April through June. Waterleaf can be found on the Appalachian Trail between Newfound and Indian Gaps. It is also known as VIRGINIA WATERLEAF. The other member of this genus you are likely to encounter is the low to middle elevation Canadian waterleaf (*H. canadense*) which has a palmately (palm leaf or hand like) lobed leaf rather than the pinnately (feather like) lobed leaf of *virginianum*. ⅜

Clinton's Lily *R. Hutson photo*

Lily-leaved Twayblade
W. Hutson photo

Galax *R. Hutson photo*

Waterleaf *R. Hutson photo*

Yellow Bead Lily
Clintonia borealis   Lily family

This small lily in the high Smokies has abundant small, green-ish-yellow flowers in May and early June hanging gracefully from stems 8 to 12 inches high. Yellow bead lily has only basal leaves. It is also known as BLUE BEAD LILY for its dark blue fruit. The Spruce-Fir Nature Trail and the Clingmans Dome Road in the vicinity of Mt. Collins are good places to see these plants. For a related species, see Clinton's lily (p. 66). ❧

Bowman's Root
Gillenia trifoliata   Rose family

This plant is a tough herb with unequal, narrow white petals pro-truding in various directions. It flowers usually in May to July, rarely in August. Bowman's root normally is found at low to medium elevations, but has been seen near mile high along the Heintooga Ridge Road. It generally can be found on roadside banks. ❧

Sweet Shrub
Calycanthus floridus   Calycanthus family

Shrubs up to 6 or 8 feet tall bear a profusion of deep maroon or brownish flowers in May and June. Magnolia-like in form, the flowers are 1-½ inches in diameter. This shrub usually has a spicy fragrance and is extremely variable, but most botanists agree there is only a single species. The blossom was used by some mountain women as a perfume substitute by secreting it on their person. Found near Sugarlands Visitor Center and near Oconaluftee Visitor Center, it generally grows on stream banks and moist, wooded slopes at elevations below 3,500 feet. Other names are BUBBY-BUSH and CAROLINA ALLSPICE. ❧

Yellow Bead Lily

W. Hutson photo

R. Hutson photo

Bowman's Root

R. Hutson photo

Sweet Shrub

W. Hutson photo

Prostrate Bluets
Houstonia serpyllifolia   Madder family

The tiny flower is usually a rich, deep blue but occasionally may be light blue or even white. The plants are only 3 to 5 inches tall, with very small leaves. They are found in moist locations from 2,000 to 6,600 feet elevation and, because of their trailing nature, usually occur in dense beds. Prostrate bluets grow along the banks of the Clingmans Dome Road and in the vicinity of the Balsam Mountain Campground from May to August. Other common names are THYME-LEAVED BLUETS, INNOCENCE and QUAKER MAIDS. ❧

Pokeweed
Phytolacca americana   Pokeweed family

This familiar and colorful plant, ranging up to 8 or 10 feet tall, flowers from May through September, often showing ripe fruits at the same time. Pokeweed is widely distributed in open areas of the lower Park elevations. This plant is very poisonous. Even though there are folk uses for pokeweed, you should not try them yourself because of the plant's toxicity. Another common name, INK-BERRY, was derived from the early settlers' use of the fruit juice as ink. Locally, it is generally known as POKEBERRY. ❧

Purple Bluets
Houstonia purpurea   Madder family

Usually 6 to 8 inches in height and with rather oval leaves, this tall *Houstonia* is fairly common on well-drained slopes from 1,000 to 5,500 feet elevation. The flowers, blooming from May to July, range from purple to lilac in color. They may be seen along the Balsam Mountain Road and at the lower edge of Andrews Bald. The plants, also known as WOODLAND BLUETS, are widely distributed through the eastern U.S. ❧

70

Prostrate Bluets

R. Hutson photo

Pokeweed

W. Hutson photo

Purple Bluets

R. Hutson photo

Wild Hydrangea
Hydrangea arborescens   Saxifrage family

This wide-ranging shrub, 3 to 4 feet tall with many clusters of white flowers, is quite common on moist, shaded slopes from the Park foothills up to 6,400 feet elevation. From May to August there are displays along both roads to Cades Cove and the Roaring Fork Motor Nature Trail. Widely distributed through the Southern Appalachians, the shrub is confused occasionally with some species of *Viburnum.* ❧

New Jersey Tea
Ceanothus americanus   Buckthorn family

Although early settlers used the leaves as a substitute for tea, thereby giving its common name, this is not a member of the tea family. The low-growing shrub, also known as RED ROOT, reaches a height of 2½ or 3 feet. It grows abundantly at the lower elevations of the Smokies, and may be found along the road to Cades Cove. The dense clusters of flowers may be seen from May to August. ❧

Goats-beard
Aruncus dioicus   Rose family

Creamy-white flowers, in plumes 3 to 5 inches in diameter and 6 to 10 inches in length, invite attention to this conspicuous plant, which grows 3 to 5 feet tall. It occurs at elevations up to 5,500 feet and may be seen along the Heintooga Ridge Road, where the flower makes an attractive display in May and June. The male and female flowers appear on separate plants, but only the botanist is able to distinguish the difference. ❧

Wild Hydrangea

W. Hutson photo

New Jersey Tea

R. Hutson photo

Goats-beard

W. Hutson photo

Purple Wakerobin
Trillium erectum var. erectum   Lily family

In May and early June, the maroon or reddish-purple flowers of this *Trillium* add interest to the trail sides in moist woods of the high Smokies. It grows along the Appalachian Trail in the vicinity of Indian Gap, Spruce-Fir Nature Trail and elsewhere in the Canadian floral zone. Because of a slightly unpleasant odor, it is sometimes called STINKING WILLIE or STINKING BENJAMIN. The white form of this species, white erect trillium (p. 24), is more abundant at lower Park elevations. ❧

Partridge-berry
Mitchella repens   Madder family

Very few flower species give us the opportunity to see brilliant fruits from last year, flowers of this year, and possibly even a young fruit from an earlier flower, all at the same time. (The picture at right is twice actual size.) Usually occurring in sizable beds, this small vine often provides a loose carpet in hemlock forests below 5,000 feet. The two tiny trumpet-shaped flowers with fuzzy petals grow side by side but produce only one twin fruit. These interesting flowers may be seen in May and June along the Cosby and Bud Ogle Nature Trails. ❧

Rough-fruited Cinquefoil
Potentilla recta   Rose family

This is an often much branched, erect, hairy, non-native, perennial. The flowers are similar to those of the common cinquefoil but the fruit is dry. Seen along roadsides, it is common in disturbed areas in May through August. ❧

Purple Wakerobin

R. Hutson photo

Partridge-berry

Heilman photo

Rough-fruited Cinquefoil

R. Hutson photo

Goat's Rue
Tephrosia virginiana   Pulse family

This 12 to 24 inch tall plant is usually found in May and June at low to mid elevations preferring open areas and dry woods. The yellowish to white petal makes for a striking contrast against the purple or pink colored petals. The characteristic pea family flower produces a slender and hairy pod. Roadsides are a good place to look for it. ❧

Yellow Buckeye
Aesculus octandra   Buckeye family

This large tree may be identified by the scaly bark, compound leaf with five large leaflets, clusters of yellow flowers at the ends of branches, and fruits (buckeyes) less prickly than those of many other buckeyes. The flowers may be seen in May and June along Park roads up to elevations of 4,000 feet. Because the wood does not split easily, it was much used by mountain people for making butter bowls and other utensils. Many people carry a buckeye as a "good luck charm." A splendid stand of these trees occurs along the Chimney Tops Trail. The national champion (136 feet tall) lies within the Park. ❧

Black Cherry
Prunus serotina   Rose family

At elevations up to 4,500 feet, many of these large trees reach diameters of 36 to 52 inches, formerly serving as lumber for valuable furniture. Flowers, appearing in May and June, may be seen along the road below Newfound Gap. So many of these trees occur below Ramsay Cascades that early settlers called the area "the cherry orchard." ❧

Mountain Ash
Sorbus (Pyrus) americana   Rose family

This small tree of the north woods, rare in the Smokies, is found this far south only at the higher elevations. It may be seen along the Clingmans Dome Road. Showy masses of white flowers appear in May and June, but the tree's greater beauty results from the shiny red fruits which appear in late August through October. The tree is so closely related to the apple tree, also of the rose family, that the two will sometimes hybridize. These trees are currently under attack by a non-native insect. ❧

Goat's Rue   *W. Hutson photo*

Yellow Buckeye   *R. Hutson photo*

Black Cherry   *R. Hutson photo*

Mountain Ash
W. Hutson photo, R. Hutson photo inset

Staghorn-sumac
Rhus typhina   Cashew family

This shrub, with a large core of pith and velvety hairy stems, grows to a height of 6 to 10 feet and is plentiful up to 4,000 feet. Slender cones of greenish-white flowers appear in May, with fruits soon turning to a reddish-brown. Flower spikes are 8 to 12 inches long. The acid fruits were used by early settlers in making a cooling drink. The two other sumacs in the Park are winged sumac (*R. copallina* winged leaf stalk) and smooth sumac (*R. glabra* smooth stems).

Four Leaved Milkweed
Asclepias quadrifolia   Milkweed family

This is the only member of this genus you are likely to encounter in the Park with leaves in whorls of fours at the middle of a solitary stem. Standing 12 to 20 inches tall it blooms in May through June. It is found at low to middle elevations and can be seen on the Round Bottom Road.

Yarrow
Achillea millefolium   Composite family

Flat clusters, about 3 inches in diameter, of white flower-heads appear in late May to July at widely scattered locations up to about 5,000 feet. Although an introduced "weed" from Europe, it is not strongly invasive since only a few plants usually grow at any one site. Yarrow's small compound leaves are almost fern-like, and its stems are from 10 to 15 inches tall.

Thimbleweed
Anemone virginiana   Buttercup family

This hairy plant usually two feet or more in height is distinguished by the cluster of fruits which resembles a thimble. The greenish white petals of the white flower are actually sepals. The leaves are palmately 3 lobed and serrate. It is found on moist shaded soils. Thimbleweed blooms along the roadside at low to mid elevations in May through July.

Staghorn-sumac *R. Hutson photo*

Four Leaved Milkweed
R. Hutson photo

Yarrow *R. Hutson photo*

Thimbleweed *W. Hutson photo*

Tulip Tree
Liriodendron tulipifera   Magnolia family

Although frequently called YELLOW POPLAR, or just POPLAR, this big tree of the Smokies is related to the magnolia and is not a true poplar. Sometimes reaching a diameter of 6 feet, it is quite abundant at elevations up to 3,500 feet. The nearest relative is in eastern Asia. Fine examples of this tree may be seen along Ramsay Cascades Trail and on the first two miles of Gregory Ridge Trail. The tulip-shaped flowers open in May and June. ❧

Spanish Bayonet
Yucca smalliana   Lily family

Known as Spanish bayonet because of its tough, sword-shaped leaves, it is also one of several plants commonly called BEAR-GRASS. Numerous creamy white flowers, 1 to 1 ½ inches in diameter, occur on branches of the 4 to 6-foot stem in late May and June. Although widely distributed in thin, rocky soil of the lower elevations, only a few plants grow at each location. It may be seen in Little River Gorge, Cades Cove and the Sugarlands Nature Trail. ❧

Blue-eyed Grass
Sisyrinchium angustifolium   Iris family

These small blue flowers appear on flattened grass-like stems up to 8 inches tall. Except for flower color, it is similar in appearance to star grass (p. 52). Blue-eyed grass is locally abundant in Little River Gorge in May and near Mile High in June and July. ❧

Rosy Twisted Stalk
Streptopus roseus   Lily family

This 12 to 30 inch tall plant is more common than twisted stalk (*S. amplexifolius*) the only other member of this genus within the Park. The flowers hang beneath its forked stem with zigzagged branches usually as a single flower from the axils of the upper leaves. The fruit is a red berry. It grows on moist slopes at high elevations such as the Appalachian Trail between Newfound Gap and Indian Gap blooming in May and June. ❧

Tulip Tree   *R. Hutson photo*

Spanish Bayonet
W. Hutson photo

Blue-eyed Grass   *R. Hutson photo*

Rosy Twisted Stalk
R. Hutson photo

Red Elderberry
Sambucus pubens   Honeysuckle family

Cone shaped clusters of cream-colored to pink flowers, on shrubs 6 to 8 feet in height, appear in May and June with bright coral or red fruits maturing in August. This species is fairly abundant in moist woods from 4,000 to 6,600 feet elevation, and may be seen along the Park road to Clingmans Dome. Although inedible, the fruits are not poisonous. A close relative, at lower elevations, is the common elder-berry with black fruits. ❧

Common Elderberry
Sambucus canadensis   Honeysuckle family

This shrub, 6 to 8 feet high, has big compound leaves on stems with extra large, pithy centers. It is the Park's only shrub having compound leaves with white flowers arranged in large, flat clusters. Flowering in June and July, it may be seen in the vicinity of Sugarlands Visitor Center. The black fruits of common elderberry were used by early settlers for making pies, jellies, and wine. It is also known as AMERICAN ELDER. Red elderberry (*Sambucus pubens*) is the only other species of this genus in the Park. Besides color, common and red elderberry can be distinguished from one another based upon a flat versus a cone-shaped flower and fruit clusters. ❧

Horse Nettle
Solanum carolinense   Nightshade family

Horse nettle is a stiff, erect herb 1 to 3 feet in height that is armed with stiff spines and has few branches. The flowers are white to purple later producing yellow berries, 1/2 to 3/4 inches in diameter. The orange center cone seen here are the anthers. It blooms at low to mid elevations from June until early September. The plant is more often found in open areas such as banks along the Little River Road. ❧

Wood Sorrel
Oxalis montana   Wood Sorrel family

The small flowers with pink stripes grow on a low plant with shamrock-like leaves. It is abundant in the higher elevations, especially as a ground cover in the spruce-fir forests where it usually appears in beds of moss. There are four other species of sorrel in the Park, all of which are also called SOUR GRASS. Wood sorrel is found along the Spruce-Fir Nature Trail. It flowers from May to July. ❧

Red Elderberry *W. Hutson photo*

Common Elderberry *R. Hutson photo*

Horse Nettle *R. Hutson photo*

Wood Sorrel *W. Hutson photo*

Sundrops
Oenothera fruticosa   Evening Primrose family

A day bloomer, the attractive yellow flowers with reddish buds appear in June and July on slightly branched plants about 2 feet tall. It is fairly abundant on well-drained slopes and open woodlands from 2,000 to 5,000 feet being more common at the higher elevations and may be seen beside the Heintooga Ridge Road and along nearby portions of Blue Ridge Parkway. ❧

Evening Primrose
Oenothera biennis   Evening Primrose family

Evening Primrose flowers about the time that the sun sets which gives rise to it its common name. Besides blooming at night rather than day, it differs from the other illustrated primrose (sundrops, *O. fruticosa*) in that it is generally taller (growing up to 5 feet tall) and has green buds. It is most frequent in open areas below 3500 feet blooming all summer till frost. Night blooming plants many times have moths as pollinators. ❧

Hawkweed
Hieracium pratense   Composite family

Also known as FIELD HAWKWEED, masses of these non-native plants with yellow flowers in June and July add beauty to the shoulders and banks of the Park roads to Clingmans Dome and to the Heintooga Overlook. Eight species of hawkweed (4 are introduced), some of which are difficult to identify, are found in the Great Smokies. ❧

Great Mullein
Verbascum thapsus   Figwort family

An introduced "weed" from Europe, this plant became well established many years ago and is now a part of the landscape along roadsides and other open areas at the lower elevations of the Great Smokies. The scattered, small lemon-yellow flowers, seen from June through August, cover the upper half of stout stems which range from 2 to 6 feet high. Because of the presence of tight-growing woolly hairs, the leaves give the false appearance of being thick and meaty. ❧

Sundrops   *W. Hutson photo*

Evening Primrose   *W. Hutson photo*

Hawkweed   *W. Hutson photo*

Great Mullein   *W. Hutson photo*

Poison Ivy
Toxicodendron (Rhus) radicans   Cashew family

Immediate recognition of this clinging vine is a must for every hiker in the Park. Few people are immune, even temporarily, from poisoning upon contact with any part of the plant (dead or alive), including its pollen or even smoke when burned. The 3 leaflets distinguish it from the 5's of the non-poisonous Virginia creeper. Poison ivy's small, greenish flowers appear from May to July, followed by fruits which are enjoyed by some birds. ❧

Flame Azalea
Rhododendron calendulaceum   Heath family

The highly popular flame azalea occurs as scattered plants and small groups throughout the Park. It flowers from April to July, depending on elevation. Fine displays may be seen on Andrews Bald and near Mile High in late June. Dramatic masses of hybrid azaleas, with colors ranging from white to red, are seen on Gregory Bald in late June and early July. Although essentially a deciduous *Rhododendron*, the azalea is known to mountain people as WILD HONEYSUCKLE. William Bartram, a botanical explorer of the 1700's, considered it to be "the most gay and brilliant flowering shrub yet known". ❧

Indian-pink
Spigelia marilandica   Logania family

This plant, 15 to 20 inches in height and rare in the Great Smokies, occurs only in limestone soils around the edges of the Park. Its flowers may be seen on the Rich Mountain Road near the Park border in May and June. The slender trumpet-shaped flowers are red on the outside, with a clear yellow on the inside or throat of the trumpet. No other species of the logania family, which is the source of strychnine, is in the Park. ❧

86

Poison Ivy

W. Hutson photo

Flame Azalea

R. Hutson photo

Indian-pink

W. Hutson photo

Purple Rhododendron
Rhododendron catawbiense   Heath family

This gorgeous shrub, blooming in June and July, is one of the most popular wildflowers of the Smokies. Its rose-purple flowers are dramatic, and the shrub is easily seen because it grows well on exposed ridges at 3,000 to 6,600 feet elevation. The usual height is 8 to 12 feet, but occasionally it too attains the size of a small tree. For example, the national co-champion growing within the Park stands 19 feet tall. Rhododendron is often intermingled with mountain laurel (page 60). Flower-clad ridges of these two shrubs are known to mountain people as laurel slicks and to botanists as heath balds. The similar dwarf rhododendron (*R. minus*, page 106) grows only 3 or 4 feet tall and is the only one of the three evergreen rhododendrons with short leaves (3 or 4 inches long). Purple rhododendron is also known as CATAWBA RHODODENDRON. ⁂

Heal-all
Prunella vulgaris   Mint family

As its name implies, it was believed to have medicinal properties at one time. This 3 to 24 inch tall plant is probably our commonest mint throughout the Park in disturbed areas. It is thought to have been a native plant but has also been introduced from overseas. Heal-all, also known as SELF HEAL and CARPENTER'S WEED, flowers all summer until frost. ⁂

Chicory
Cichorium intybus   Composite family

Chicory is a branched, slender, introduced, herb with a composite head of blue (rarely white or pink) ray flowers. It is found along roadsides and in old fields at lower elevations. The root is used as an adulterant of coffee. It flowers all summer. ⁂

Clingmans Hedge-nettle
Stachys clingmanii   Mint family

This mint is characterized by the 4 angled stem having spreading, rather stiff hairs on the angles and none or few on the flat surfaces. It is usually about 3 feet tall, with pink, irregular flowers. Clingmans hedge-nettle is usually found at higher elevations such as the Clingmans Dome Road and in the vicinity of the Heintooga Picnic Area in July and August. This plant and Clingmans Dome were named after Thomas Lanier Clingman, a confederate general and U.S. senator. ⁂

Purple Rhododendron *R. Hutson photo*   **Heal-all** *R. Hutson photo*

Chicory *W. Hutson photo*   **Clingmans Hedge-nettle**
R. Hutson photo

Crown Vetch
Coronilla varia   Pulse family

This is a perennial ascendant or trailing vine, normally 1 to 2 feet long but occasionally longer, with pinnately (like a feather) compound leaves and no tendrils. The flowers have both pink and white parts and are borne in spherical clusters throughout the summer. The pods are four angled and linear. This non-native occurs at low elevations and can be seen on the Gatlinburg Bypass and Little River Road. ❧

Purple Fringed Orchid
Platanthera (Habenaria) psycodes   Orchid family

Dozens of exquisite little orchids in clusters at the top of a 12 to 20 inch stem makes this plant strikingly beautiful. Although not abundant, it occurs throughout the Park in wet, acid soils at elevations of 2,500 to 6,500 feet. They may be seen in June and July along the road to Clingmans Dome and the road to the Heintooga Overlook. ❧

Passion-flower
Passiflora incarnata   Passion-flower family

Also known as WILD APRICOT and MAYPOP, this is a vine up to 10 feet in length. The unusual, fringed flowers are seen from June to September. Edible fruits mature from July into October. Its habitat is disturbed areas such as Cades Cove and Cherokee Orchard along fences and the roadside. This was Tennessee's State Flower until 1933 when the cultivated Iris replaced it. According to legend, the parts of the flower resemble the instruments of Christ's crucifixion, the corona representing the crown of thorns; the stamens and pistil, the nails of the Cross; the petals and sepals, the faithful apostles. This and the yellow passion-flower, *P. lutea*, are the Park's only members of a large family of tropical plants. ❧

Fly-poison
Amianthium muscaetoxicum   Lily family

Moderately rare, fly-poison occurs at scattered Park locations in open woods at elevations from 2,500 to 5,300 feet. It is abundant at the Heintooga Picnic Area. The flowers appear in June and July on stems 2 to 3 feet tall. Arching basal leaves, with unusual V-shaped ribs, are 15 to 20 inches long. As the name implies, the plant has poisonous properties. ❧

Crown Vetch *R. Hutson photo*

Purple Fringed Orchid
W. Hutson photo

Passion-flower *W. Hutson photo*

Fly-poison *W. Hutson photo*

Mountain Myrtle
Leiophyllum buxifolium   Heath family

This small shrub is restricted mainly to the edges of laurel slicks from 4,000 to 6,500 feet elevation in the Smokies. The star-like flowers, ranging from white to pale pink, appear mostly in June but sometimes earlier. The plant, only 15 to 20 inches tall, grows in dense beds. Myrtle Point on Mt. Le Conte was named for this beautiful shrub. This plant is also widely known as SAND MYRTLE but here in the Smokies Mountain Myrtle seems more appropriate. ❧

Queen Anne's Lace
Daucus carota   Parsley family

Also known as WILD CARROT, this 1 to 5 foot tall, non-native plant is a familiar sight along roadsides and other disturbed areas of the Park up to an elevation of about 4,000 feet. It may be seen in Cades Cove, where it blooms throughout the summer and early autumn. Most of the flowers are white, in flat heads or umbels, but on rare occasions they may be pale purple. ❧

Butterfly-weed
Asclepias tuberosa   Milkweed family

These orange-colored flowers are a conspicuous part of the landscape on dry soils in open areas up to about 2,000 feet elevation. They appear in Cades Cove and along the western end of the Park from June through August. The stiff plant, up to about 2 feet high, is also known as CHIGGER WEED and ORANGE MILKWEED. There are seven other milkweeds in the Smokies. ❧

Mountain Myrtle

W. Hutson photo

Queen Anne's Lace

W. Hutson photo

Butterfly-weed

W. Hutson photo

Yellowwood
Cladrastis kentukea (lutea)   Pulse family

This somewhat rare tree, with large clusters of flowers hanging
gracefully from its branches, is a thing of beauty in June.
Unfortunately, major blooms do not occur every year. It is thinly
scattered at elevations from 1,500 to 3,500 feet and may be seen on
trails in the Cosby Campground area and the Cove Hardwood
Nature Trail. The leaves and flowers, with their white corollas,
resemble wisteria. Other common names are CHITTUM and GOPHER-
WOOD, which legend tells us was used by Noah in building his ark.
Early settlers obtained yellow dye from the wood. ❧

Indian-pipe
Monotropa uniflora   Wintergreen family

An odd plant, Indian-pipe is found in thinly scattered clusters
throughout the Smokies and may be seen from June through
August along trails to Mt. Le Conte and beside the Spruce-Fir
Nature Trail. Having no chlorophyll, it lives off the roots of other
plants. The stem is 5 to 8 inches tall, with a single, nodding white
or occasionally light pink or blue flower at the top. Another common
name is GHOST PLANT. The only other species of this genus in North
America is pinesap (p. 114). ❧

Indian Paintbrush
Castilleja coccinea   Figwort family

The showy color of this plant lies in the reddish-orange bracts, the
bases of which are light green. Small tubular flowers, also light
green in color, are almost hidden between layers of bracts. The plant,
sometimes known as SCARLET PAINT-CUP, is 12 to 18 inches tall, with
clusters of flowers and bracts about 1½ inches long. It may be seen
along the roadside near Mile High in June and July. ❧

Black Cohosh
Cimicifuga americana   Buttercup family

The slender, wand-like clusters of white flowers, on plants 4 to 8
feet tall, have been described as "tapering candles to light
Nature's church." They appear in June and July and are widely distributed at elevations up to 3,000 feet. They grow along the Cove
Hardwood Nature Trail, Grotto Falls Trail, and the Gregory Ridge
Trail. Other common names include BLACK SNAKE ROOT, RATTLETOP,
and MOUNTAIN BUGBANE. ❧

Yellowwood *R. Hutson photo*

Indian-pipe *W. Hutson photo*

Indian Paintbrush *W. Hutson photo*

Black Cohosh *Heilman photo*

Wild Potato Vine
Ipomoea pandurata   Morning Glory family

This native long trailing vine gets its name from a large starchy root which can weigh as much as 9 to 25 pounds. There are two native and three exotic members of this genus in the Park all with the funnel shaped flowers growing along roadsides at low elevations. Wild potato vine can generally be distinguished from the other morning glories in the Park based upon its heart shaped leaves with a lavender or pink throated white flower more than 1½ inches long. It blooms all summer and can be seen on the Gatlinburg Bypass and entwined in the fences on the Cades Cove Loop Road. ❧

Trumpet Honeysuckle
Lonicera sempervirens   Honeysuckle family

This slender woody vine, bearing the most brilliant of our honeysuckle flowers, occurs at lower elevations and on fences in nearby areas. It may be found in June along the road to Cherokee Orchard. CORAL HONEYSUCKLE is another common name, and locally it is also known as WOODBINE. It is not a vigorous pest like the Japanese honeysuckle (*L. japonica*). ❧

Coreopsis
Coreopsis major var. stellata   Composite family

Also known as TICKSEED or WOOD TICKSEED, this species grows to a height of about 3 feet and is common in open, well-drained Park areas at elevations from 1,500 to 5,000 feet. It may be found in Little River Gorge, where it flowers from June to August. The leaves, which occur as opposite pairs, are so deeply cut that they resemble 6 whorled leaves. The less common (*var. major*) has pubescent (hairy or downy) stems and leaves. ❧

Wild Potato Vine

W. Hutson photo

Trumpet Honeysuckle

W. Hutson photo

Coreopsis

W. Hutson photo

Blue Haw
Viburnum cassinoides   Honeysuckle family

Blue haw, one of the eight *Viburnum* species in the Great Smokies, is a 10-foot shrub fairly abundant at elevations up to 6,000 feet. It may be seen on Andrews Bald and near Alum Cave Bluff. The white flowers appear in June, with fruits maturing in August and September. Other common names include WILD RAISIN and ARROW-WOOD. The red haw (*Crataegus*) is not related. ❧

Canada Mayflower
Maianthemum canadense   Lily family

This small herb, only 3 to 6 inches tall, is fairly abundant in moist, cool woodlands from 3,000 to 6,000 feet elevation. It flowers in June and July and occurs along the Appalachian Trail between Newfound and Indian Gaps and in the Heintooga Overlook and Andrews Bald areas. Another common name is WILD or FALSE LILY-OF-THE-VALLEY. ❧

Ox Eye Daisy
Chrysanthemum leucanthemum   Composite family

This non-native flower gives bright color to the roadsides and fields in April to July. Standing 1 to 3 feet in height, it can be found in open areas at low to mid elevations such as along the Little River Road and Cades Cove. The white ray flowers surrounding the yellow disc flowers are quite striking. ❧

Blue Haw

W. Hutson photo

Canada Mayflower

R. Hutson photo

Ox Eye Daisy

R. Hutson photo

Flowering Spurge
Euphorbia corollata   Spurge family

The tiny flowers are unisexual and borne in clusters resembling flowers. The white or pinkish "petals" are actually petal shaped appendages. If the 1 to 3 foot stem is broken, it exudes a milky white sap as does many of the other plants in this family. The flowers are found in open dry areas and bloom in summer giving rise to another common name SUMMER SPURGE. ❧

Cardinal Flower
Lobelia cardinalis   Bluebell family

These brilliantly colored flowers are abundant at the edge of streams and in swampy soils up to about 2,500 feet. Watch for them in wet pasture areas along the Cades Cove Loop Road. They grow to a height of 3 to 5 feet, with flower clusters measuring 10 to 12 inches in length, and bloom from June through August. Four other lobelias, blue or purple in color, are found in the Park. ❧

Mountain Mint
Pycnanthemum species   Mint family

Although the flower is not very spectacular, the white of its flower and leaves is an eye catcher at a distance. Some of these mints were called SNOW ON THE MOUNTAIN by local people. They bloom all summer at low to mid elevations. ❧

Rugel's Indian Plantain
Cacalia rugelia   Composite family

Although not known to exist anywhere except in the High Smokies, this plant, formerly known as RUGEL'S RAGWORT, is locally abundant in the spruce-fir forests on peaks such as Mt. Le Conte and Clingmans Dome and can be seen along the Spruce-Fir Nature Trail. The creamy-tall clusters of tiny flowers on plants up to 15 inches tall may be seen from June to September. The heads lack rays and are unusually large and compact. The split or bifurcated ends of each stigma curve in opposite directions. ❧

Flowering Spurge   *R. Hutson photo*

Cardinal Flower   *R. Hutson photo*

Mountain Mint   *R. Hutson photo*

Rugel's Indian Plantain
R. Hutson photo

Blackberry
Rubus species   Rose family

Flourishing at all elevations, the many species of blackberry are important as wildlife food and ground cover in the Smokies. Blackberries are among the first plants to become established after forest fires, "blow-downs," or other disturbances. The woody arching canes reach a height of 4 to 8 feet the first year, bear flowers and fruit the second year, and then die, remaining upright for another year or so. After early summer flowering, fruits ripen from early July through August, depending upon the elevation. Canes of *R. canadensis*, a species common at higher elevations, have few spines or thorns. ❧

Basswood
Tilia heterophylla   Linden family

These inconspicuous creamy white blossoms, suspended from the convex side of a curved bract, are seen in June. Bees turn to these flowers as an important source of honey. Also known as WHITE BASSWOOD, LINN or LINDEN, the tree may be seen along the Cove Hardwood Nature Trail and along the road to Cades Cove. Before the tree reaches maturity a dozen or so young basswood sprouts appear around its base. A few of these sprouts grow to maturity after the central, or parent, tree dies. Resourceful early settlers twisted the pliable inner bark from young basswoods to make rope for their corded beds, for plow-lines and parts of harness. ❧

Mountain Camellia
Stewartia ovata   Tea family

The large white flowers of this small tree, when seen from a distance, sometimes cause it to be mistaken for late flowering dogwood. It is quite rare, and the only member of the tea family in the Smokies. The mountain camellia, also known as MOUNTAIN STEWARTIA, blooms in June and early July and is found in rich soils at 1,000 to 2,000 feet elevation. Locals have also called it SUMMER DOGWOOD due to the flowering time and similarity of the bloom to flowering dogwood (p. 20). Near the Sugarlands Visitor Center are several mountain camellia trees. ❧

Blackberry

R. Hutson photo

Basswood

W. Hutson photo

Mountain Camellia

W. Hutson photo

Sourwood
Oxydendrum arboreum   Heath family

This normally small tree is conspicuous for its graceful sprays of white bell shaped flowers from June to August and for the extreme brilliance of its red leaves in autumn. It can however reach large sizes. The national champion tree growing within the Park, for example, stands 96 feet tall. Sourwood is abundant up to about 3,500 feet. The pale gray fruits, which remain through the summer, are often mistaken for flowers. It is our only member of the heath family that is truly a tree. The nectar from its flowers produces the choicest of all wild honey. Sourwood may be seen on Gatlinburg Bypass and the lawn of the Sugarlands Visitor Center. ❧

Swamp-thistle
Cirsium muticum   Composite family

Large numbers of butterflies, especially black swallow-tails, are attracted to the numerous blue-purple flowers of this showy native plant. The flowers, on branched plants 4 or 5 feet tall, appear from June into September. Swamp-thistle has very few spines. It may be seen in disturbed areas below 5,500 feet, as along the Heintooga Ridge Road. It is one of six thistles (4 natives and 2 exotics) to occur in the Park. ❧

American Chestnut
Castanea dentata   Beech family

At one time this was one of our larger, more numerous and important forest trees, the nuts being used by wildlife as well as humans. Its destruction represents one of the greater ecological disasters to have occurred. The bark was valuable for leather tanning and the wood for construction. Blooming in June, the male flowers are white and borne in long finger-like clusters near the base of which are small inconspicuous female flowers. The fruit is very prickly especially after drying and contains, on average, 3 nuts which are said to be taster than the European varieties. A blight introduced to this country from overseas has virtually eradicated this tree from its former range. Hopefully on-going research will find a solution. Old stumps exceeding 12 feet in diameter bear silent witness to their former grandeur. Trees mature enough to bear fruit are now difficult to find but root-sprouts are seen in various woodlands at elevations between 1500 and 3200 feet. They can be recognized by their narrow spear-shaped, serrated leaves. ❧

Sourwood *W. Hutson photo*

Swamp-thistle *R. Hutson photo*

American Chestnut Stump
R. Hutson photo

American Chestnut Flowers
W. Hutson photo

Bush Honeysuckle
Diervilla sessilifolia   Honeysuckle family

This low-growing shrub, only 3 or 4 feet tall, is rather common in forest openings or exposed ridges at the higher elevations of the Smokies and nearby mountains, such as along the famous Appalachian Trail. The yellow flowers are present from late June through August. The leaf blades have no leafstalk and are attached directly to the shrub's branches. ❧

Dwarf Rhododendron
Rhododendron minus   Heath family

This is a small shrub, similar to the purple rhododendron (page 88) but having smaller leaves with rusty undersurfaces. The flowers have green spots on their pink to white corollas. It flowers in June and July at various elevations. Spectacular displays can be seen on narrow ridges such as Myrtle Point on Mt. Le Conte. ❧

Rattlesnake Plantain
Goodyera pubescens   Orchid family

This orchid, also known as DOWNY RATTLESNAKE PLANTAIN, is characterized by its white-veined basal leaves peculiar to the genus. It has small white flowers in July and is found on moist, wooded slopes at elevations up to 4,000 feet, such as along the Cosby Nature Trail, Porters Creek Trail, or between Cherokee Orchard and Rainbow Falls. Most stems reach a height of 10 to 15 inches. Of the two species which occur in the Park this is the more common, the other being dwarf rattlesnake plantain (*G. repens var. ophioides*) whose flower spike is one sided or spiraled rather than being densely cover by flowers ❧.

Purple Gerardia
Agalinis (Gerardia) purpurea   Figwort family

The flowers of this species so closely resemble those of two related species, slender gerardia (*A. tenuifolia*) and narrow-leaved gerardia (*A. setacea*), that a minute examination is necessary to distinguish them. Flowers of all three species may be seen in the meadows and edges of woodlands of Cades Cove, from August through October. The profusely branching plants, about 15 inches tall, are semiparasitic on grass roots. ❧

Bush Honeysuckle *R. Hutson photo*

Dwarf Rhododendron
R. Hutson photo

Rattlesnake Plantain *R. Hutson photo*

Purple Gerardia *R. Hutson photo*

Ramp
Allium tricoccum   Lily family

An annual festival near the Smokies is held to celebrate this
"sweetest tasting, and foulest smelling, plant that grows". In
early spring its tubers have a pleasant taste of sweet spring onions,
but an obnoxious garlic-like odor persists for two or three days
afterward. The broad leaves, resembling those of lily-of-the-valley,
appear in April on moist, wooded slopes at elevations of 1,500 to
4,000 feet. Leaves disappear completely by late June, and greenish-
purple flower clusters appear shortly afterward. In Northern states
this plant is known as WILD LEEK. ❧

Teaberry
Gaultheria procumbens   Heath family

A tiny shrub, only 6 or 7 inches tall, the teaberry is prevalent in
acid soils of oak and pine forests below 5,000 feet. It may be
seen along the Smokemont and Sugarlands Nature Trails and on
many of the heath balds of the mid-altitudes. Late June and July
are the flowering season. Before the days of synthetics, this plant
was a source of wintergreen (or teaberry) flavor. Other common
names are CHECKERBERRY, WINTERGREEN, and MOUNTAIN TEA. ❧

White Rhododendron
Rhododendron maximum   Heath family

The white to shell-pink flowers of this species appears in mid
June through July. It grows in deep forests, along streams, and
in moist soils at all Park elevations. ROSEBAY RHODODENDRON is
another common name. ❧

Ramp

W. Hutson photos

Teaberry

W. Hutson photo

**White
Rhododendron**

W. Hutson photo

Hairy Alumroot
Heuchera villosa   Saxifrage family

Hairy alumroot is a 8 to 32 inch tall hairy plant with acutely lobed maple like leaves. It has hairy stems and flowers clustered on branches. The name Alumroot refers to the astringent properties of the underground stem. It can be found in summer along shaded bluffs at low to mid elevations. ❧

Spiderwort
Tradescantia subaspera var. montana   Spiderwort family

The spiderworts are popular garden flowers. This particular wild species stands 12 to 32 inches tall and has leaves reminiscent of a grass. It can be found though out the park at low to mid elevations, such as the Round Bottom Road. The flowers, which take on various shades of blue, appear in June and July. ❧

Michaux's Saxifrage
Saxifraga michauxii   Saxifrage family

Reddish-green leaves and stem—and spatulate leaves that are strongly toothed—help identify this species. Usually growing to a height of 10 to 12 inches with a range of 4 to 20, it prefers wet bluffs and boulders at elevations from 2,500 to 6,000 feet. It is predominant at the higher elevations whereas the related species brook lettuce (p. 22) does at the lower elevations. In the vicinity of Alum Cave Bluff the flowers, with a yellow spot on three of the petals, appear from late June through September. This plant is named for Andre Michaux, an early botanical explorer of the Southern Appalachians. Another common name is LETTUCE SAXIFRAGE. ❧

Purple-flowering Raspberry
Rubus odoratus   Rose family

This gracefully arching shrub, with rose-purple flowers resembling single roses, reaches a curved length of 6 to 8 feet. In the Great Smokies, it is found at elevations of 1,500 to 3,500 feet, but its range extends northward to Canada. The red fruits, highly acid and quite seedy, form a single layer around the central core contributing another common name, THIMBLEBERRY. Early settlers often used the berries for making jam and jelly. The two other "raspberries" in the Park have compound rather than simple leaves. They are the American red raspberry (*R. idaeus var. canadensis*), also with red fruits, and the black raspberry (*R. occidentalis*) with black fruits and thorns. The purple flowers of *R. odoratus* appear near Chimneys Picnic Area from July to September. ❧

110

Hairy Alumroot *R. Hutson photo*

Spiderwort *R. Hutson photo*

Michaux's Saxifrage *R. Hutson photo*

Purple-flowering Raspberry
R. Hutson photo

Touch-me-not
Impatiens pallida   Touch-me-not family

Known also as PALE JEWEL WEED and SNAPWEED, this plant grows to a height of 3 to 5 feet in moist or wet soils at 2,000 to 3,500 feet. When the mature pods are touched, the fruits "explode," hence "touch-me-not." The related spotted jewel weed or orange jewel weed (*I. capensis*), usually at lower elevations, has orange flowers with brown spots. Both species bloom in July and August along Sugarlands Nature Trail. They are hummingbird favorites. ❧

Grass-pink
Calopogon tuberosus (pulchellus)   Orchid family

This beautiful orchid grows to a height of 12 to 18 inches. A tall, slender, grass-like leaf reaches about the same length. Preferring moist, open areas at elevations from 1,500 to 4,500 feet, it occurs in the vicinity of Sugarlands Visitor Center and near Fontana Village. The flowering time is July. It is somewhat selective about pollinators as it requires a bee or butterfly heavy enough to bend the upper part of the flower holding the pollen down so that the pollinator comes into contact with the stigma projecting from the bottom of the flower. ❧

Black-eyed Susan
Rudbeckia hirta   Composite family

This plant, conspicuous in flower, is one of six members of the genus in the Great Smokies. It may be seen at the edge of Indian Gap and elsewhere at elevations of 900 to 5,000 feet. Growing mostly on open slopes, the black-eyed susan reaches a height of about 3 feet, blooming in July and August. It is a native of the prairies which has migrated east. A closely related species is the wild golden glow (p. 118). ❧

**Touch-me-not,
Spotted left
Pale right**

*R. Hutson photo
W. Hutson photo far right*

Grass-pink

W. Hutson photo

**Black-eyed
Susan**

W. Hutson photo

Crimson Bee-balm
Monarda didyma — Mint family

Also called OSWEGO TEA, this bright-flowered mint usually occurs in beds of a few feet to several feet in diameter. It likes rich, wet, acid soils from 2,500 to 6,500 feet in elevation, and is quite showy near the entrance to Chimneys Picnic Area. The plant attains a height of 2 to 3 feet, and blooms in July and August. The leaves have a pleasant odor. The members of this complex genus occurring in the Park can be separated to some degree based on color, crimson bee-balm being crimson, wild bergamot (*M. fistulosa*) pink, basil balm or horse mint (*M. clinopodia*) white to pink, and purple bergamot or purple bee-balm (*M. media*) dark purple/reddish-purple. Some people feel *M. media* is really a crimson bee-balm hybrid or color variant. ❧

Turk's-cap Lily
Lilium superbum — Lily family

The Latin name *superbum* is certainly appropriate for this lily of the high Smokies. With its beautiful brown spotted orange petals, it truly is superb. Several inverted flowers hang from supporting branches of stately plants that grow 6 to 10 feet tall. The leaves are in whorls about 10 inches apart. An accessible location to see it is along the road to the Heintooga Overlook where it blooms from July to August. It is related to the Carolina lily (*L. Michauxii*). They can generally be differentiated on the basis that Carolina lily will have no more than 4 flowers all borne from the very top of its stem (umbel) where as Turk's-cap lily's flowers are borne along its stem at different levels (raceme). ❧

Pinesap
Monotropa hypopithys — Wintergreen family

This parasitic non-green plant has several small, drooping, tan or red flowers at the end of a stem 5 to 8 inches tall. This is in contrast to the single flower of the related Indian-pipe (p. 94). Fairly common in deciduous woods below 3,000 feet, pinesap is sometimes observed along the Cades Cove Nature Trail where it flowers from July to September. ❧

Tall Bellflower
Campanula americana — Bluebell family

The flower has flaring blue petals rather than the typical bell shape which distinguishes this bluebell from others. It is the only member of this genus besides southern harebell (p. 120) that one is likely to encounter in the Park. The leaves on this 1½ to 6 foot tall plant are 2-6 inches long and usually toothed. It is found in moist, shaded soils that are not very acid at low to mid elevations throughout the Park in July and September. ❧

Crimson Bee-balm   *W. Hutson photo*

Turk's-cap Lily   *R. Hutson photo*

Pinesap   *W. Hutson photo*

Tall Bellflower   *R. Hutson photo*

Virgin's Bower
Clematis virginiana   Buttercup family

Also known as COMMON CLEMATIS and TRAVELER'S JOY, this climbing vine, at times 30 or 40 feet long, is quite common in open areas at elevations up to about 2,000 feet. The numerous creamy white flowers abundant in July to September often almost obscure the foliage. In autumn the feathery fruits are almost as attractive as the blossoms and easy to spot as you drive along. It may be seen in Cades Cove and around Oconaluftee. ❦

Joe-pye-weed
Eupatorium maculatum   Composite family

"Weed" is the wrong name to apply to such a stately plant. The name QUEEN OF THE MEADOW used by early settlers seems more appropriate. Huge clusters of pink-purple flowers, atop coarse stems up to 12 or 15 feet high, are especially attractive, in both form and color, when seen against a blue sky. The flowering season is July through September. Cades Cove or the Sugarlands Visitors Center is a good place to view the plants, which like moist soils up to 3,000 feet. ❦

False Foxglove
Aureolaria (Gerardia) flava   Figwort family

Growing to about 3 feet tall, this stiff herb flowers in July and August. It is relatively abundant in dry woods at elevations up to 2,500 feet and may be seen along Sugarlands Nature Trail, Laurel Falls Trail and in Cades Cove. Another common name for this plant is YELLOW GERARDIA. ❦

Virgin's Bower

W. Hutson photo
R. Hutson photo far right

Joe-pye-weed

W. Hutson photo

Foxglove

R. Hutson photo

Loosestrife
Lysimachia quadrifolia   Primrose family

The only loosestrife with whorled leaves in the Smokies is this species which is fairly common on dry slopes up to 5,000 feet elevation, such as at Mile High on the road to the Heintooga Overlook. The whorled leaves give rise to the common name WHORLED LOOSESTRIFE. Flowers occur in July and August on plants ranging up to 3 feet tall. Another species in the Park is fringed loosestrife (*L. ciliata*) whose major leaves are opposite. ❧

Wild Golden-glow
Rudbeckia laciniata   Composite family

The bright yellow flowers with short, cone-shaped centers occur on plants 3 to 6 feet tall at almost all elevations in the Smokies. One location is along the highway near Smokemont, where they flower from July to September. It is also known as GREEN-HEADED CONEFLOWER. ❧

Appalachian Avens
Geum radiatum   Rose family

Also known as MOUNTAIN AVENS, this extremely rare plant is restricted to a few high peaks of the Smokies and nearby mountains, where it flowers in July and August. Park regulations prohibit picking or otherwise disturbing all plants, but there is an additional reason for not tampering with this beautiful flower - its marked scarcity. The closest relative is Peck's avens of the White Mountains. ❧

Yellow Fringed Orchid
Platanthera (Habenaria) ciliaris   Orchid family

Words fail to due justice to this exquisite orchid. The beautiful clusters of numerous small, fringed flowers, either yellow or orange, occur along the upper part of stems that range from 1 to 3 feet tall. A given plant normally does not bloom every year. Its habitat is acid, shady soils at elevations from 2,000 to 4,000 feet. Although widely scattered, this orchid may be found from July through August in pine woods near Cades Cove, along the road to the Heintooga Overlook and along the Bullhead Trail. It is closely related to purple fringed orchid (p. 90). ❧

Loosestrife　　　*R. Hutson photo*

Wild Golden-glow　　　*R. Hutson photo*

Appalachian Avens　　　*W. Hutson photo*

Yellow Fringed Orchid
W. Hutson photo

White Snakeroot
Eupatorium rugosum var. roanense   Composite family

There are about 13 snakeroots in the Smokies. This species is abundant on shaded slopes at elevations from 1,500 to 6,000 feet. From July to September it grows in profusion along the trail to the Clingmans Dome Tower. The plants are 3 to 5 feet tall. Snakeroot is poisonous to cattle, and, through milk, to humans. ❧

Southern Harebell
Campanula divaricata   Bluebell family

The small, blue flowers (seen here at four times life size) are bell-shaped with a long extruding style. They usually droop from horizontal branches, appearing in mid-summer to early fall. It is probably the most common bluebell in the Park and stands 8 to 20 inches tall. While considered to be a low to mid elevation species, a large display occurs on a rock face along the Heintooga Ridge Road. ❧

Grass of Parnassus
Parnassia asarifolia   Saxifrage family

Definitely not a grass despite its common name, this species is limited to the Southern Appalachians. In the Smokies it is found in moist or wet spots from 4,500 to 6,500 feet elevation, and may be seen on Mt. Le Conte. The white fluted petals with green stripes, appear in August and September on stems 5 to 8 inches tall. ❧

120

White Snakeroot

W. Hutson photo

Southern Harebell

R. Hutson photo

Grass of Parnassus

R. Hutson photo

Crane-fly Orchid
Tipularia discolor   Orchid family

Found at low to mid elevations, this rather inconspicuous orchid, which normally is about a foot tall but can be up to two feet in height, is quite dainty when viewed close up. After the deciduous trees have lost their leaves in the fall, this tiny plant puts out a single leaf to absorb sunlight all winter. In spring the leaf withers away and nothing more is seen of the plant until it blooms in July through September. Like putty root (p. 62), some locals referred to it as RESURRECTION ORCHID since the flower appears after the death of the over wintering leaf. These orchids can be seen along the Sugarlands Nature Trail. ❧

Starry Campion
Silene stellata   Pink family

This pretty white flower is 20 to 40 inch tall. It grows in rich woods at low to middle elevations. It can be distinguished from the other campions in the Park as it generally has at least a few whorled leaves at the middle of its stem. Note how the flower petals are fringed rather than simply cleft. Starry campion blooms in July through September. It is a relative of fire pink (p.62). ❧

Hercules'-club
Aralia spinosa   Ginseng family

The creamy-white flowers of July and August and the reddish-blue fruits of September and October are equally spectacular. A stout, thorny stem often rising to 15 feet is topped with a cluster of flowers up to 20 inches in diameter. The national champion in the Park stands 60 feet tall. Good displays of this shrub occur between Fighting Creek Gap and Sugarlands Visitor Center. Another common name is DEVIL'S WALKINGSTICK. ❧

Mountain St. John's-wort
Hypericum graveolens   St. John's-wort family

In the Smokies, this yellow flower, which appears in July and August, is found only at the higher elevations. At 5,500 to 6,600 feet, such as on Mt. Le Conte and Clingmans Dome, it is fairly common. The plants are 15 to 18 inches in height. Some botanists insist that this species and *H. mitchellianum* are the same. ❧

Crane-fly Orchid   *R. Hutson photo*

Starry Campion   *R. Hutson photo*

Hercules'-club   *R. Hutson photo*

Mountain St. John's-wort
R. Hutson photo

Nodding Pogonia
Triphora trianthophora   Orchid family

This relatively rare orchid grows in moist, open, acid soils up to 3,500 feet elevation in the Great Smokies. The erect, branched stems, 6 to 10 inches tall, bear pink "nodding" flowers in mid-summer. A few of these flowers have been discovered near Cherokee Orchard and along the road to Heintooga Overlook. This is also known as THREE BIRD ORCHID. ❧

Mistflower
Eupatorium coelestinum   Aster family

This 1 to 3 feet tall plant has an unusual blue flower head. It grows at low to mid elevations and blooms in July through October. Mistflower can be seen in the vicinity of the Sugarlands Visitors Center. ❧

Heart-leafed Aster
Aster cordifolius   Aster family

Its heart shaped leaf gives this plant its name. Aster is a difficult genus and this one can be confused with *A. lowrieansus*, which generally has winged petioles (leaf stalks). Heart-leafed aster is one of the common fall asters that can be found at all elevations. It is 2 to 5 feet tall and blooms August through November. This particular specimen was on the Roaring Fork Motor Nature Trail. ❧

Summer-sweet
Clethra acuminata   White Alder family

The only member of this tropical family to occur in the Park, summer-sweet is a shrub that occasionally reaches 15 feet in height. In July and August, its numerous spikes of white flowers appear in Little River Gorge and elsewhere on moist slopes and along Park streams from 1,500-5,500 feet elevation. Because early settlers used the dried seeds as a substitute for black pepper, they called it SWEET PEPPERBUSH. That, however, is a name applied by botanists to *C. alnifolia*, which grows on the coastal plains and not in the Smokies. Another name for this plant is MOUNTAIN PEPPER-BUSH. ❧

Nodding Pogonia *W. Hutson photo*

Mistflower *R. Hutson photo*

Heart-leafed Aster *R. Hutson photo*

Summer-sweet *R. Hutson photo*

Rose-pink
Sabatia angularis   Gentian family

A nother common name for this flower, appropriately, is MEADOW BEAUTY. It flowers in August and September, and the angled stem may range from a few inches to 2 feet in height. Rose-pink is generally rare, but is fairly common in a few scattered, open areas having a sandy soil at elevations from 1,000 to 3,000 feet. It may be seen along the Cades Cove side of the Rich Mountain Road and other areas which are rich in limestone. ❧

Closed Gentian
Gentiana linearis   Gentian family

A lso known as LINEAR LEAVED GENTIAN, this rare narrow-leaved species grows on wet, rocky slopes from 5,000 to 6,000 feet elevation. Extremely rare south of Maryland, it is found along the Alum Cave Trail and alongside the Blue Ridge Parkway near the Smokies. It grows 12 to 15 inches tall and blooms in August and September. Its broad-leaved relative, mountain gentian (p. 132), is fairly abundant in the Park. The bee that pollinates the closed gentian pulls the petals apart to enter. ❧

Monkshood
Aconitum uncinatum   Buttercup family

I n the Great Smokies the attractive and rare monkshood is found mostly in open locations of the spruce-fir forests, and may be seen on Mt. Le Conte. This species is restricted to the Southern Appalachians. The plants, which prefer moist or wet soils, attain a curved length of 5 to 6 feet. Large numbers of blue-purple flowers bloom in August and September. ❧

Filmy Angelica
Angelica triquinata   Parsley family

D uring late summer, this unique species is one of the most abundant and conspicuous wildflowers along the last 2 or 3 miles of the Clingmans Dome Road. Much of its interest lies in the complex form of the large clusters of flowers, on plants 3 to 5 feet in height. A favorite of bees, they congregate on the flowers and are interesting to watch as they go about their work. The plant is probably poisonous. ❧

Rose-pink   *R. Hutson photo*

Closed Gentian   *R. Hutson photo*

Monkshood   *R. Hutson photo*

Filmy Angelica   *W. Hutson photo*

Stiff Gentian
Gentiana quinquefolia   Gentian family

Its profusion of flowers helps distinguish this species from the other four gentians in the Smokies. As many as 50 flowers appear on each branched plant. The slightly "open" flowers, on plants 12 to 18 inches tall, range from violet-blue to lilac. They are plentiful along the road to the Heintooga Overlook in August and September. ❧

Great Lobelia
Lobelia siphilitica   Bluebell family

Usually a deep, rich blue, this species occasionally may be pink or even white. Note the distinctive white stripes seen here on the underside of the corolla. The stiff stem is 2 to 3 feet in height, with flowers appearing in August and September. It is fairly common in moist locations at lower elevations of the Park and is found in Cades Cove. The plant was once thought to be effective in the treatment of syphilis. Another Park species, Indian tobacco (*L. inflata*), is used in preparations to curb the cigarette habit. ❧

Pink Turtlehead
Chelone lyonii   Figwort family

A fairly abundant plant at higher elevations of the Smokies, turtlehead is not known to occur north of Tennessee and North Carolina. It may be seen on Mt. Le Conte and the Clingmans Dome Road. The stems reach a height of 15 to 24 inches. The shape of the flowers, which appear in August and September, clearly suggest the common name. If one will gently press the sides of the flower, the "turtle's mouth" can be made to open. Two varieties of the white turtlehead, *C. glabra*, a highly variable species also occur in the Smokies. ❧

Tall Ironweed
Vernonia gigantea (altissima)   Composite family

One of the Park's most brilliant autumn flowers is produced by this impressive plant that grows 5 to 9 feet tall. It is quite abundant in the open spaces of the Park's foothills at low elevations. Another species which is rarer in the Smokies, New York ironweed (*V. noveboracensis*), is principally found in Cades Cove. The two can be distinguished as New York ironweed has more flowers (30+) on each flower head. Both bloom in August until October. ❧

128

Stiff Gentian *W. Hutson photo*

Great Lobelia *R. Hutson photo*

Pink Turtlehead *R. Hutson photo*

Tall Ironweed *R. Hutson photo*

Curtis' Aster
Aster curtisii   Composite family

This is one of the most abundant and most beautiful species of aster found in the Great Smokies. Flowers, ranging from white to rich blue, on stiff, branched stems up to 3 feet tall, appear from late August to winter. Occurring in well-drained soils from 1,800 to 5,500 feet, they are plentiful in the vicinity of Mile High. Botanists find it difficult to identify positively many of the over 20 aster species found in the Park. ❧

American Holly
Ilex opaca   Holly family

This evergreen tree, with a spiny-margined leaf, is fairly common up to about 4,000 feet in the Smokies. Sometimes reaching a trunk diameter of more than 2 feet and a height of 80 to 90 feet, it may be seen along the Laurel Falls Trail and Hyatt Lane in Cades Cove. The sexes are separated there being male and female trees. The small, creamy-white flowers of May and June are seldom noticed, but the tree is famous for its bright red fruits of autumn and early winter. Since the berries provide winter food for many birds, the use of twigs and berries for Christmas decorations is disturbing conservationists. ❧

White Wood Aster
Aster divaricatus   Aster family

This common aster on trailsides at low to mid elevations and occasionally higher is fairly distinctive for an aster. The blooms, which appear in late summer till frost, have white ray flowers around a yellow to brown center disk. It has serrated heart shaped leaves and stands 12 to 30 inches tall. White wood aster can be found on the Appalachian Trail between Newfound and Indian Gaps. ❧

Downy Aster
Aster pilosus   Aster family

This hairy fall aster is quite pretty standing 2 to 5 feet tall. Blooming from September until November, it can be found at low elevations preferring open sunny areas such as roadsides and old fields. ❧

Curtis' Aster   *R. Hutson photo*

American Holly   *Kohout photo*

White Wood Aster   *R. Hutson photo*

Downy Aster   *R. Hutson photo*

Erect Goldenrod
Solidago erecta   Composite family

Erect goldenrod has an erect, essentially branchless, stem with rather small, cylindrical clusters of yellow flowers. Standing 2-4 feet tall it can be seen along roadsides, old fields, and lower woodlands. It flowers in late summer and early fall and is one of many goldenrods in the Park some of which are difficult to identify without careful study of the entire plant. Many goldenrods grow in Cades Cove. ⚜

Obedient Plant
Physostegia virginiana   Mint family

Sometimes called FALSE DRAGONHEAD, it is usually more than three feet tall, the stem has paired lance shaped narrow leaves. The rather long flower clusters when twisted, do not return to their original positions, hence the name obedient. Obedient plant is generally restricted to moist soil at low elevations with underlying limestone blooming in August and September. ⚜

Mountain Gentian
Gentiana decora   Gentian family

The flowers are borne in tight clusters in the top part of the plants. The attractive pleated, tubular, corollas are bluish striped with paler hues. It is interesting to watch bees make their way in and out of these flowers by prying apart the petals. Mountain gentian can be found along Rich Mountain Road in September and October. It is the most common species of the gentians within the Park and grows in many other areas, such as the Appalachian Trail between Clingmans Dome and Silers Bald. ⚜

Ladies' Tresses
Spiranthes cernua   Orchid family

One needs a magnifying glass to fully appreciate the beauty of the tiny white flowers arranged in spirals around the foot-high stem of this late-blooming orchid. Also known as NODDING LADIES' TRESSES, it grows along the trails, such as the one to Laurel Falls, and in other relatively open spaces up to 6,000 feet. The flowers, which are said to resemble a woman's braided hair, occur from August through October. Next to it is shown the low to mid elevation species slender ladies' tresses (*S. lacera var. gracilis*) whose flowers have a green center. The other two ladies' tresses occurring in the Park are little ladies' tresses, (*S. tuberosa*) which has the smallest petals (about 0.1" long) and a pure white flower, and early ladies' tresses (*S. vernalis*) which has flowers with a yellow center and is the first to start its blooming season. ⚜

Erect Goldenrod *W. Hutson photo*

Obedient Plant *R. Hutson photo*

Mountain Gentian *W. Hutson photo*

**Nodding Ladies'
Tresses**
R. Hutson photo

**Slender Ladies'
Tresses**
R. Hutson photo

Goldenrod
Solidago glomerata   Composite family

This particular goldenrod, one of 19 goldenrods found in the Smokies, is both golden and rod-like. Species occurring at lower elevations have spreading flower clusters. This species, known as SKUNK GOLDENROD, is fairly abundant in a few open spaces at elevations of 5,000 to 6,000 feet, as on Thunderhead. Its usual height is about 3 feet, with flowers appearing in August and September. The heavy pollen of the goldenrods does not carry very far in the air, and seldom if ever causes hay fever. The ragweed, which blooms at the same time, is usually the hay fever culprit. ᵛ

Hearts-a-bustin'
Euonymus americanus   Staff-tree family

A beautiful erect shrub 5 to 10 feet tall, hearts-a-bustin' is found throughout the lower and intermediate elevations, usually near a stream. The early summer small flowers are inconspicuous, but the plant compels attention in early autumn when its wine-colored pods burst open, revealing brilliant orange-red seeds. Common names include STRAWBERRY BUSH, SWAMP DOGWOOD, SPINDLE BUSH ARROWWOOD, WAHOO, and a dozen others. A relative, trailing wahoo or running strawberry bush (*E. obovatus*), is also found in the Smokies. The flowers or fruits of hearts-a-bustin' may be seen along Sugarlands Nature Trail and near Oconaluftee Visitor Center. ᵛ

Witch-hazel
Hamamelis virginiana   Witch-hazel family

From late October into early January the cream-yellow petals of witch hazel are conspicuous along the streams in the lower elevations of the Smokies. The flowers are easily seen because they appear after defoliation of the witch-hazel bushes. Since the flowers appear so late in the year, one might ask if this is really the last plant of the season to bloom. Perhaps it is first for the next season, since fruits resulting from these flowers do not develop until the following summer. Witch-hazel is found in Little River Gorge and along the road leading to the Bud Ogle Nature Trail. ᵛ

134

Goldenrod

W. Hutson photo

Hearts-a-bustin'

W. Hutson photo
R. Hutson photo inset

Witch-hazel

R. Hutson photo

Index

138

141

142